The Hollywood Sign

The Hollywood Sign

Fantasy and Reality
of an American Icon

Leo Braudy

Yale UNIVERSITY PRESS   NEW HAVEN & LONDON

Published with assistance from the foundation established in memory of
Philip Hamilton McMillan of the Class of 1894, Yale College.

Yale University Press books may be purchased in quantity for educational, business, or
promotional use. For information, please e-mail sales.press@yale.edu (U.S. office) or
sales@yaleup.co.uk (U.K. office).

Set in Janson type by Integrated Publishing Solutions.
Printed in the United States of America.

The Library of Congress has cataloged the hardcover edition as follows:
Braudy, Leo.
The Hollywood sign : fantasy and reality of an American icon / Leo Braudy.
p.   cm. — (Icons of America)
Includes bibliographical references and index.
ISBN 978-0-300-15660-7 (alk. paper)
1. Motion picture industry—California—Los Angeles—History.   2. Motion pictures—
United States—History.   3. Hollywood (Los Angeles, Calif.)—History.   4. Los Angeles
(Calif.)—History.   5. Hollywood Sign (Los Angeles, Calif.)—History.   I. Title.
PN1993.5.U6B674 2011   384'.80979494—dc22   2010043473

ISBN 978-0-300-18145-6 (pbk.)

A catalogue record for this book is available from the British Library.

ICONS OF AMERICA

Mark Crispin Miller, Series Editor

Icons of America is a series of short works written by leading scholars, critics, and writers, each of whom tells a new and innovative story about American history and culture through the lens of a single iconic individual, event, object, or cultural phenomenon.

Contents

Prologue

The Hollywood sign may be unique among American icons. It is a landmark whose white block letters are familiar around the world as the prime symbol of the movies. Day after day tourists with cameras wander into surrounding Griffith Park or troll up and down the streets of the Hollywood Hills, looking to position themselves for the best possible angle on the sign. More than any other sight in Los Angeles, the Hollywood sign in the background of your photo proves you were really there. To moviegoers and so many others, the sign represents the earthly home of that otherwise ethereal world of fame, stardom, and celebrity—the goal of American and worldwide aspirations to be in the limelight, to be, like the Hollywood sign itself, instantly recognizable.

But in contrast with the Statue of Liberty or Mount Rushmore, the Hollywood sign doesn't depict a human image, nor is

The Hollywood sign as seen from Beachwood Drive

it in the form of an immediately familiar object, like the Liberty Bell or the Washington Monument. It may signify a place, but it's not the place itself, as is Valley Forge or the battlefield of Gettysburg. Nor does it commemorate a moment in time, as do the submerged USS *Arizona* in Pearl Harbor or the memorial to the Oklahoma City bombing.

Instead it is a group of letters, a word on the side of a steep hill that, unlike so many other cherished sites, cannot be visited, only seen from afar. Its essence is almost entirely abstract, at once the quintessence and the mockery of the science of signs itself. Resembling the urge it inspires to the secular form of transcendence we call fame, the Hollywood sign embodies the American yearning to stand out of the landscape. It reflects the impulse to performance and singularity that has been a part of the American psyche since our country first appeared, unprecedented, on the world stage in the late eighteenth century. At the same time, its ubiquitous place in the eyes and digital cameras of the world shows how thoroughly that urge and impulse has pervaded so many cultures other than our own. As a character in the German film *Kings of the Road* says, "The Americans have colonized our subconscious." The Hollywood sign immediately evokes the movie capital it looms over, and the configuration of its letters has been imitated by cities and towns everywhere to trumpet their own imitative uniqueness. But it is its mere wordness, its lack of any tangible image that would pin down and restrict its meaning, that particularly invites the veneration and admiration of every hopeful candidate for fame, regardless of race, creed, color, or national origin, if only for the snapshot of a moment.

In its religious origins, an icon, as its Greek meaning indicates, was a resemblance, a portrait, worshiped not in itself but as a pathway to another reality. Thanks to its contemporary use in the computer world, however, the word *icon* has been applied to an enormous number of instances, sometimes almost losing its basic meaning as a visual symbol that refers to something else, by likeness or analogy. When *icon* is applied to a person, it has come to mean a legend, a superstar beyond normal categories of fame. Even in the series this book is part of, we have historical icons (the Founding Fathers), book icons (*Gone with the Wind*), and

A family puts itself in the picture with the sign

food icons (the hamburger). Basically *icon* has come now to mean something special, something easily recognizable, something that has a distinguished or at least notorious history, something essential to the idea of the United States of America.

But the original meaning of *icon* continues to be powerful. Like every icon, modern and ancient, the Hollywood sign has both a physical and a metaphysical life, reaching beyond itself to unspecified wonders in an invisible world of potential and possibility. Instead of enhancing our sense of patriotism and history, as do so many other American icons, the Hollywood sign focuses on our dreams and our inner life, for good or ill. Where other icons are anchored in the times and national events they celebrate, the Hollywood sign floats above its setting and its circumstances, open to anyone's interpretation.

Even by these expanded definitions, the Hollywood sign is a strange sort of icon. It isn't an image that looks like or refers to something called Hollywood; it is the name itself. Yet people everywhere recognize it as the symbol of whatever "Hollywood" might be—with whatever ambiguity is part of that meaning. The Hollywood sign might therefore seem to be the perfect symbol of modern celebrity, the sign that celebrates itself, spelling out "Hollywood" for all the world to see.

Can there be icons before they are pictured and those pictures are widely disseminated? In great part the Hollywood sign has become an icon because so many people have seen it that way, and it would mean little without all those who photograph it or want to be photographed near it. Iconized, canonized by innumerable repetitions, its enhancing aura makes people feel better about themselves. Unlike the presidential faces on Mount Rushmore or the goddess image of the Statue of Liberty, the blandness of the sign, its lack of representing anything but itself, makes it easier to project upon and associate with. To call the Hollywood sign an icon is to recognize the icon as a distillation of meaning, an unchanging essence that pervades the shifting world it seems to represent, hovering above the streets—sometimes even above the clouds—and the day-to-day specifics of the industry called "Hollywood."

Where did this urge, this strange pilgrimage to a collection of white sheet-metal block letters, come from? What is the point of seeing the sign or being photographed nearby? Few know much of its history. Some may recall that it once read "Hollywood-land," and others have also perhaps heard the often garbled story of the actress Peg Entwistle, who, it is said, disappointed in her search for Hollywood success, committed suicide by jumping from the "H" in 1932. Over the years the letters of the sign have been parodied endless times, including alterations sacred and profane: HOLLYWEED in 1976 to celebrate a new California law that changed the charge for possession of marijuana from a felony to a misdemeanor; HOLYWOOD in 1976 to celebrate the Easter sunrise service at the Hollywood Bowl; PEROTWOOD to promote the presidency of Ross Perot in 1992 and 1996; and various permutations of USC and UCLA for their annual crosstown football grudge match. Even in 2010, when developers threatened to subdivide the land surrounding the sign—which the City of Los Angeles had carelessly never managed to acquire for itself—the sign, seemingly so permanent and otherwise so open to the eyes of the world, had plenty of mysteries to explore.

■

From my home in Los Angeles there are several ways to get to the Hollywood sign, even though there are also many streets with prominent signs stating "No Access to the Hollywood Sign." Tired of the congestion, neighbors have petitioned City Council to stop the tourists in search of the sign from traipsing down streets from which you can only glimpse it, not really get near it.

Although it has existed since the early 1920s as an actual object, the Hollywood sign as the goal of tourist pilgrimage is in fact a comparatively recent phenomenon. But it makes up for its short life in the frequency of its reproduced images, from every possible angle, hardly as artistically resonant as Hokusai's *Thirty-six Views of Mt. Fuji*, although much more widespread in its influence. Like our relation to movie stars themselves, the relation of the tourists with their cameras to the Hollywood sign is a complex mixture of intimacy and self-enhancement. Seeing the sign lets you know you are in Hollywood, that special place. Photographing it enhances your sense of your own identity, like glimpsing a movie star in the supermarket. As a character on the animated cartoon show *King of the Hill* says when introduced to a celebrity, "You must remember me. I've seen you on television." We know them, we think, even though they don't know us, just as the HOLLYWOOD over the shoulder of visitors lends an aura of status and prestige because they are near it. Instead of looking at the Liberty Bell or the Lincoln Memorial and appreciating their importance and the history they represent, we look at the Hollywood sign and it looks back at us, enlarging our sense of our prestige by its symbolic aura.

Was any icon immediately accepted as such? The way significance gathers on some revered objects is always a function of the time in which it is "seen." Even Stonehenge wasn't of interest to

The Hollywood sign from the west with the dog park below

more than a few antiquaries until, in the seventeenth century, it became a symbol of arguments over the relative political power of the king and parliament. Manufactured icons especially always seem inadequate or ersatz at first: The Statue of Liberty and the Eiffel Tower were heavily criticized when they initially appeared; the Liberty Bell did not receive its common name until it was almost a hundred years old. Part of the accumulation of feeling and celebration around an icon is based not on a fixed meaning but on the number of ways it can be viewed and interpreted. We might call this shifting meaning the icon's framing, as it rotates through the different perspectives of those who look at it, photograph it, and buy images of it on postcards. But the Hollywood

The Hollywood sign firmly planted on Mount Lee with the
communication towers behind

sign again differs from most other icons because its original purpose was so transitory—an advertisement for a real estate development. Only over the years has it accrued the multiple meanings
now laid upon it. Like one of Marcel Duchamp's "readymades,"
ordinary objects turned into art by being placed inside the frame
of a museum or art gallery, the Hollywood sign gathers its meanings from where it is placed and what people think of it, more
than what it is in any intrinsic way.

Originally a grandiose sort of billboard, the Hollywood sign's
material existence became only a casual springboard to its later
significance. Like the Eiffel Tower, also at first slated to be only
a temporary structure, an object on the landscape that was de-

signed to be impermanent made over the years a permanent impression on the national and international imagination. Even though the sign we now see is not the original sign at all, it still carries the same weight of meaning. Just a few of the film studios in the past were physically within the confines of a town called Hollywood. But the sign has come over the years to stand for them all, wherever they are. The story of the Hollywood sign is therefore inextricably intertwined with the story of Hollywood itself, how a business largely run by immigrants for an immigrant audience, filmmakers who had run away from the East Coast to escape legal pressures or to seek a climate more conducive than New York or Chicago to year-round filmmaking, created in a few short decades a world-embracing industry of dreams.

ONE

Hollywood Before "Hollywood"

As our streetcar entered Hollywood that morning [in 1914], we found
it the same dilapidated suburb it had been when we lived in Los Angeles
[in 1906]. Our main purpose in ever going there had been to ride to the end
of the line and take lunch at the Hollywood Hotel, a rambling edifice painted
the same dun color as the hills, with a veranda where elderly seekers after
sunshine, mostly from the Middle West, sat in big red chairs and rocked
their uneventful lives away. Across from the hotel was a shoddy business
district; there were a few bungalows interspersed with vacant lots, and
that was all. Nobody dreamed a day was close at hand when that one
word, Hollywood, would express the epitome of glamour, sex,
and sin in their most delectable forms.
—ANITA LOOS, *A Girl Like I*

Before there was a sign that represented Hollywood, there had
to be a Hollywood that it referred to. Few of the movie people
who would later be so identified with Hollywood were very impressed with the Los Angeles suburb when they first saw it.
Charlie Chaplin in his autobiography comments that the road
from Los Angeles to Hollywood was "almost impassable," and
when an early member of the Automobile Club of Southern California predicted that the trip from Los Angeles to Hollywood
would only take a few hours by car, he was greeted with incredu-
lous laughter. The Hollywood Hotel at the corner of Highland

and Prospect, built in 1903 to house potential real estate buyers, Chaplin called "a fifth-rate . . . barnlike establishment," barely tolerated by those staying there in order to be near the embryonic studios. Cecil B. DeMille similarly spoke of "a long drive through the straggling outskirts of Los Angeles" before arriving at "the somnolent village of Hollywood." Most of the early moviemakers preferred to stay, if they could afford it, in the Alexandria Hotel in downtown Los Angeles (built in 1906 and still standing). Even there, Frances Marion, a transplant from San Francisco who was to become the highest paid screenwriter of silent films and, along with Anita Loos, the most prolific, complained of the provincialism of Los Angeles (let alone Hollywood) and noted with disdain the crude rooming house signs proclaiming "No Jews, actors, or dogs allowed."

At the time that Chaplin, DeMille, and Marion arrived, ten or fifteen years after its origins in the mid-1890s, the movie business was still considered a lower-class entertainment or a passing fad, in any case nothing that respectable people should pay attention to. Films were shown in nickelodeons and were rarely more than two reels (about twenty minutes) in length, usually shorter. Some companies, like Biograph and Vitagraph, were beginning to be prominent, but the industry itself was in a period of organizing and reorganizing that would not settle down until the beginnings of the studio system in the mid-1920s. Except for a few fledgling companies setting up shop in southern California to evade the thugs and enforcers of the Edison Trust, and a few of the major companies coming west for the winter, the major bases of filmmaking were in the New York, Chicago, and Philadelphia areas.[1] The names of individual performers were generally left out of any credits, in part because the production companies didn't want to give them any reason to ask for higher salaries. As far as most Angelenos of the time were concerned, anyone who worked in this marginal business was called a "movie," a general term of contempt for anyone who worked in the "flickers."

Until 1880 the population of Los Angeles was small. Starting with forty-four people in the original eighteenth-century town, by then it had finally broken through ten thousand. The nineteenth century had been marked by the gradual absorption of the old Mexican California into the new California, helped along immeasurably by the defeat of Mexico in the war of 1846–48, the discovery of gold at Sutter's Mill in northern California in 1848, and the entry of California into the union in 1850. Especially in southern California the influence of the old families called the Californios was undermined by the subsequent swallowing up of Spanish land grant areas into the new American state. Only six years after statehood, the Los Angeles Board of Land Commissioners approved the city's title to four square leagues, whose northwest boundary is still marked by a plaque in front of the old Monogram Studios on Sunset Boulevard (now the television station KCET) and across the street from where the sets for D. W. Griffith's *Intolerance* later rose. Growth was slow. A decade and a half later, in 1873, a township map west of Los Angeles proper described the approximate Hollywood area as "cactus and under-brush." It was a sleepy time when a failed development called Morocco had yet to turn into Beverly Hills.

Slowly Los Angeles was being transformed from a minor military outpost on the fringes of the Spanish empire into an American city. The Gold Rush at first helped the city's economic expansion by putting a premium on southern California–raised beef cattle that could be sold to the hungry miners of the north. But by mid-century this business was superseded by competing beef from other parts of the country with better transportation access to the Bay Area. Wheat, vineyards, and citrus groves followed, along with some even less plausible crops, like coffee, tea, and silk farming. This was also the era when promoters had high hopes for eucalyptus trees until it became clear that the California version was not a hardwood crop, and so the trees were relegated to being wind breaks and atmospheric junior partners of the picturesque palms, with even more of a tendency to turn into firecrackers in a fire.

Finally, to help create the beginnings of a modern economy for the area, came the railroad. Or the railroads, it would be more accurate to say, beginning in 1869 with the first transcontinental link—Council Bluffs, Iowa, to Alameda, California, in the north—and gathering steam as the century wore on. In 1871 the Southern Pacific went south from Sacramento to Los Angeles and then east to the Colorado River, ready to link with other railroads in the Southeast and Midwest. The West Coast was being connected directly to the East and the Midwest. Not incidentally the railroads, with their large land grants surrounding the right of way, were also lavishly promoting the opportunities for settlement at every station along the route, publishing tourist-oriented books, and generally making southern California what one historian has called "perhaps the best-advertised portion of the country during the third quarter of the [nineteenth century]."

In the late nineteenth century, then, a new gold rush was on, with often less tangible riches in sight, especially the fantasy of a better and healthier life than the one left behind. The southern California climate lured farmers, herders, health seekers, tourists, and fortune hunters generally, especially from the Midwest. Competitive fares went down so far that at one time you could get from Kansas to Los Angeles for only a dollar. Thanks to the railroads, the first major building in most towns was not a church or a town hall but a hotel for land buyers.

In 1883 the Southern Pacific completed a New Orleans–Los Angeles line, and within a short time Harvey H. Wilcox and his wife Daeida arrived. Harvey had been born in New York state, raised in Michigan, and married his first wife Ellen in Ohio, where he dealt in real estate. After moving to Topeka, Kansas, his wife died. A few years later he married Daeida, from Hicksville, Ohio. In 1884 they moved to Los Angeles and later bought land in the Cahuenga Valley, just north of a town called Colegrove, which had been developed from a five-hundred-acre chunk of Rancho La Brea by a former senator from California, Cornelius Cole, who had christened it with his wife's maiden name. Cole had been deeded the land by Major Henry Hancock, a Civil War veteran and early surveyor of Los Angeles, for his successful defense before the Supreme Court of Hancock's claim to a Spanish rancho.

In 1885 the Atchison, Topeka & Santa Fe Railroad also arrived in Los Angeles, linking the city to Chicago. The reputation of southern California as a place for retirement and health, again heavily promoted by the railroads, in particular the Southern Pacific, was beginning to grow. The north may have lured migrants looking for gold, but the south, especially Los Angeles, chiefly brought people who hoped to retard the effects of old age and sickness. By 1890 the population of Los Angeles was four and a half times its 1880 size (from 11,183 to 50,395), and small towns had sprung up everywhere along the railroad right of way. Meanwhile, Harvey H. Wilcox had filed a grid map for his twenty-five blocks (120 acres) of an area called Hollywood in 1887 and started placing ads to drum up (respectable) buyers. It was the same year a developer named George Shatto bought Catalina Island and began building the town of Avalon to attract affluent tourists. A land boom was on in southern California, railroad companies were giving tours that included all-you-can-eat picnic lunches and discounted tickets, and the Los Angeles Chamber of Commerce (founded in 1888) was eagerly publishing promotional pamphlets and sending railroad cars around the country with exhibits aimed to swell the urge to migrate, or at least to visit. In one of the first of many short-lived booms, prices were skyrocketing and people made tidy profits flipping houses and property. In the early 1890s the discovery of oil in the Los Angeles basin supplied another financial inducement—black gold to compete with the white gold of the north.

Where "Hollywood" as a name came from is shrouded in mystery, not the last unverifiable story to be told about the place. Depending on the source, the name was suggested to Daeida Wilcox by a woman she met on a train who owned a similarly named estate near Chicago; or it was proposed by her neighbor Ivar Weid; or by the developer H. J. Whitley and his wife while on their honeymoon; or it referred to the Hollywood Hotel in Long Branch, New Jersey, a favorite retreat of Chicago society, or, for the pious, it alluded to the Mass of the Holy Wood, celebrated by Padre Junipero Serra in the area later to become the Hollywood Bowl—a story either ignored or unverified by most of his biographers.[2]

The speculations are endless, but the fact remains that Hollywood is the name on the grid submitted by H. H. Wilcox in 1887, laid out, like Los Angeles itself, in accordance with the Continental Survey for agricultural land, with major intersections every mile. Still other Hollywood etymologists associate the name with the red berries and green leaves of the California Toyon holly—a link corroborated in 1904 when local residents persuaded the Los Angeles City Council to rename Griffith Peak at the top of Vermont Canyon as Mount Hollywood. Colonel Griffith had given the land to Los Angeles in 1896 but was still interested in developing it, especially for a funicular railway that would run to the top. The year before, however, Griffith had shot his wife in the eye during an unfortunate bout of alcoholic jealousy in the presidential suite of the Arcadia Hotel in Santa Monica. She had saved herself further harm only by jumping out the window and landing on a first-floor awning that broke her fall. His name now less respectable, even to label a piece of chaparral-covered geography, Griffith's proposal was rejected. As one of the park commissioners concluded, Mount Hollywood was more appropriate "for the reason that so many holly berries grow there."

■

Several miles away from the growing city of Los Angeles, over those "almost impassable" roads, what kind of Hollywood did Harvey and Daeida Wilcox expect to build? Wilcox, almost thirty years older than his wife, had lost the use of his legs through polio. It might be reasonable to assume that he, like so many others, came West at least in part for health reasons. But the Wilcoxes were prohibitionists as well, and there's more than a tinge of the white Christian temperance utopia in their founding of Hollywood—another version of the California dream. In the late nineteenth century the desire to retreat to a better, safer place was in the air. It was a time when the newspapers were filled first with scare stories of the Reconstruction South and then with similarly induced panics about the surge of immigrants from eastern and southern Europe who were entering and changing the large urban areas of the East Coast. Economically the Long Depression of 1873–79 was still a fresh memory, and recent events like the Chicago Haymarket Riot of 1886 no doubt continued to justify the decision to leave the shadow of any big city for a more godly, pastoral life, in all senses of the words. The health to be gained in California not only meant bodily health; it might also mean what some considered to be moral and spiritual health, a purified world without the pollutions, material and human, of the crowded cities of the East.

Sociological theory in the 1890s was similarly fascinated with what was seen as the growing threat to "civilization" of crowds and masses of people. Heavy industry, alcohol, potentially contaminating minorities, and crime were to be banished so that individual and social health could reign supreme. Even the growing Progressive politics of California bought into some of those fears by emphasizing the need for eugenics, a theory of racial renewal first named in 1883 and popularized by Francis Dalton, a cousin of Charles Darwin. Early feminists like Charlotte Perkins Gilman, who wrote *Herland*, about a utopian world without men, while living in Pasadena, as well as Jack London, the northern California writer, who championed Nietzschean ideas about a super race, slip back and forth across the line between what might be called positive eugenics (improving health and general human character) and negative eugenics (getting rid of those considered substandard). Until Nazism began to give eugenics a bad name, it was extremely popular in both the Midwest and the West. California in 1909 passed a forced sterilization bill, and a traveling exhibit called *Eugenics in New Germany*, sponsored by the German government, drew crowds in Pasadena in 1934, at a time when sterilization for criminal behavior was legal in twenty-seven states.

No documentation ties the Wilcoxes explicitly to such views, but utopias of all sorts were part of the atmosphere in southern California, and would continue to be. In 1891, the year Harvey Wilcox died, advertisements for Hollywood and its surrounding areas proclaimed the "frostless foothills," where citrus crops were bountiful. A few years later, to hammer home the significance of this edenic world as a mecca for the rest of the country, the orange crates headed to the sickly East began to be adorned with stylized images of sunny California—eternal sunshine, beautiful women, and luxurious nature.

After Harvey Wilcox's death, Daeida remarried and continued to take a strong hand in the development of Hollywood. Further benefiting like many western cities from the migrations induced by the Panic of 1893, Los Angeles was continuing to grow, and Hollywood with it, incorporating as a town in 1897. Then in 1903 it became a municipality "of the sixth class" (with a population between five hundred and three thousand), its original boundaries having been expanded by annexation, including a southern chunk between Sunset Boulevard and Fountain Avenue.

Now an official community of its own, Hollywood continued

to try to keep its distance from the big city to the east, busying itself with laying out streets and curb lines, although as yet few houses could boast sidewalks in front of them. Even though it now had municipal status, Hollywood's DNA still came from the agricultural world of the Midwest. There would be grand houses and no doubt some smaller ones as well, but there should be land for orchards and other kinds of planting—enough space for people to feel they were still in the countryside, however restrained and organized. As one of the early promotional ads proclaimed, along with photographs of palatial homes, leafy boulevards, and lush gardens: "The City of Hollywood is noted for its many beautiful homes, fine paved streets and pleasant drives." Other ads took up the practicalities: "Choice Building Lots in the Holly Tract now platted and ready for sale at $150 to $400 per lot on easy terms. A Beautiful Home . . . A Splendid Investment." (The prices quoted are equivalent to about $3,500 to $10,000 today, still a great bargain.)

Hollywood's prohibitionist roots were quickly visible as well. Ordinance Ten of the newly incorporated town prohibited the sale of liquor in public places except for medical purposes and dispensed by a licensed pharmacist. (In 1911 the Women's Christian Temperance Union would hold its state convention in the Methodist Church at the corner of Hollywood Boulevard and Ivar Avenue.) Ordinance Eleven, passed a month later, prohibited public drunkenness and disorderly conduct. Later ordinances banned pool rooms, shooting galleries, bowling alleys, slaughter-

An early brochure lures new residents to Hollywood, stressing its bucolic plantings, spacious building plots, and luxurious homes (Courtesy of hollywoodpictures.com)

houses, glue factories, soap factories, gas works, tanneries, and other such morally and physically polluting businesses. Nor were the aesthetics of this miniature eden ignored: additional ordinances regulated the ability of homeowners "to willfully injure, disfigure, girdle or destroy" shade and ornamental trees; prohibited "camping or traveling outfits" to park themselves and their animals in the streets; and created penalties for those who threw rubbish in streams and other watercourses.

Daeida Wilcox, who by 1894 was married to Philo J. Beveridge, the son of a former governor of Illinois and one of the backers of a new streetcar line, also had a central role in creating Hollywood society. One of her most successful early ventures had been to lure a French artist named Paul de Longpré to settle there. De Longpré was a watercolorist, born in Lyon to a family of artists, who had first come to prominence in his native country as a child prodigy, showing in the Salon of 1876 and later at the International Exposition of 1889. His subject matter was flowers, which he depicted on fans and textiles and in full-scale paintings. In 1890, in the wake of the failure of the Comptoir d'Escompte bank due to copper speculation, he had moved to New York, where his paintings, according to the *New York Times*, became "much in vogue." In 1898, broken down from overwork and what he described as an operation on an abscess "near the base of his brain," he decided to move to Los Angeles, "sated with the culture of the Old World, and with the restless ambition of New York." In 1901 Daeida Wilcox, with a promise of free land (as she had already offered to churches) and a less stressful setting, enticed him to Hollywood, while his paintings were being shown in exhibitions in San Francisco, Chicago, New York, and St. Louis. In 1902 he built a Moorish mansion that quickly became a prime tourist sight for visitors from Los Angeles and beyond, where they could visit his house and gardens, and perhaps even buy his work. The warmth and sunlight of southern California was thus hardly a unique discovery of the movie business, and touring the distinctive mansions and gardens of the Los Angeles area was a popular pastime for the twenty thousand or so people a year that wintered there beginning in the 1890s.

De Longpré, like many of the other millionaire retirees or active businessmen who came to settle in those early years, was part of the Hollywood world of art and privilege that seems to have been Daeida's dream to create. With his continental cachet, he became such an integral part of the scene that when the town was incorporated, there was a movement to change the name of Prospect Avenue to De Longpré Boulevard. De Longpré himself ended the controversy by what the *Los Angeles Times* called a "manly letter" withdrawing his name from consideration. Prospect Avenue in due course became Hollywood Boulevard, and de Longpré's name was given instead to a narrow east–west street between Sunset and Fountain.

That de Longpré's specialty was flowers complemented the image of edenic innocence and abundance already present in the numerous citrus orchards in the "frostless" zone at the base of the foothills, and gave a native Hollywood prestige to a style represented in the East by the natural forms that marked Art Nouveau, Tiffany lamps, and La Forge stained glass. Daeida Wilcox Beveridge died in 1914, and at her death there was still little about the small Los Angeles suburb she helped found that in any way signified hospitality to the world of movies, with its socially marginal and immigrant roots. For at least a brief time the early settlers of Hollywood tried to keep it that way.

The Christian temperance utopia envisioned by the Wilcoxes was hardly the only such ideal community to put down roots in this area. Sprawling still on the southwestern slopes of Beachwood Canyon is a complex of homes linked by winding roads originally called the Krotona community. Named for the sixth-century B.C. Italian site of the utopian community founded by Pythagoras, Krotona was first planted in the Hollywood Hills in 1912 by the Theosophist Society. In addition to homes, parks, and centers for study and meditation, it included at its spiritual core the Grand Temple of the Rosy Cross, a Moorish-inspired complex on Vista del Mar Street that is now an apartment house. That same year, 1912, L. Frank Baum, the author of *The Wizard of Oz*, built a home he called Ozcot just off Hollywood Boulevard, where he wrote all of the later Oz books and, like Paul de Longpré, gained a reputation for his flower garden.

Baum and his wife had been members of a Theosophical Society in Chicago and, while there is little evidence of his connec-

tion with the Krotona community, some of his critics have no-
ticed theosophical imagery and ideas in the Oz books, and the
Temple of the Rosy Cross was just a few blocks away from Ozcot.
In the 1930s, continuing the alternate spiritualist and occult
traditions of the area, came the Vedanta settlement of Swami
Pravadananda on Vine Street Hill, celebrated in Christopher
Isherwood's memoir *My Guru and I*. It is still housed on a street
near Cahuenga Boulevard called Vedanta Terrace, where the
temple buildings include a large Craftsman house and a miniature Hindu temple, just under the shadow of the freeway that
nicely isolates this still-living segment of the old Hollywood utopian sensibility from the speed of new developments.

Baum was also involved in several film ventures, less success-
fully than his fantasy-world and Hollywood neighbor, Edgar
Rice Burroughs, the creator of Tarzan. But whatever movie production was taking place in the Los Angeles area, with few exceptions, tended to be far from Hollywood. Trying to construct
a direct line between the Hollywood of the past and the Hollywood of the present day, historians of the early film business like
to trace the first studios to open there and argue over what was
the first film to be shot within the boundaries of what Frances
Marion in 1918 was still calling "a drowsy little village." But in a
scattered and fledgling industry of small entrepreneurs, there
was no premeditated effort to make Hollywood the center of the
West Coast film business, let alone the American film business
generally. If anyone had told the film pioneers that this desert

suburb of scattered mansions, small bungalows, and pepper trees would turn into a world-famous place, they would have thought it was a joke. Until World War I, the film business was primarily an East Coast enterprise, and Hollywood, much less often than the hills of Edendale and Glendale or the beaches of Venice and Santa Monica, was a sometimes convenient, but hardly permanent, stopping place. Cecil B. DeMille, heading to Arizona to make *The Squaw Man* for Famous Players–Lasky in 1913, decided that Flagstaff didn't really look enough like the West and wired New York for extra money to go on to Los Angeles, the end of the line, where by chance a barn was for rent on Selma Avenue near Sunset Boulevard toward the southern boundary in Hollywood.

For whatever reasons—the increasing appetite of American audiences for new films, the weakening of the Edison Trust's reach, the economic advantage of being able to shoot year round in inexpensive sets or on location—1909 had been the first year of an East Coast awakening to the possibilities of shifting at least some filmmaking operations to the sunnier West. But for the most part the migrating studios set up shop anywhere but in Hollywood. Considering the tone of high-mindedness set by Daeida Wilcox Beveridge, as well as the prohibitions of the new town government, they avoided the place for obvious reasons. After a year testing the photogenic possibilities of downtown Los Angeles, the Selig Company from Chicago came out in 1909 to establish a permanent facility in Edendale, along the north-

the years in southern California take up a small portion of the book, and there is no mention of Hollywood beyond a reference to the Hollywood Cemetery (now called "Hollywood Forever"), where both Coles, like the Wilcoxes, are buried.[3]

In 1909, when Cole was 87, with still 15 more years to live until his death at 102 in 1924 (still the greatest longevity of any U.S. senator), Colegrove, later referred to as South Hollywood, was annexed by Los Angeles. In 1910, by contrast, Hollywood voted to accept the more dignified alternative of consolidation with its larger neighbor to the east, less distant thanks to the coming of the Pacific Electric Railway's "red cars" down the renamed Prospect Avenue, now Hollywood Boulevard. The kind of isolated grandeur and moral purity envisioned by the Wilcoxes in founding Hollywood, and protected by the need to travel for a few hours from Los Angeles over bumpy dirt roads, was beginning to crumble under the pressure of new floods of migrants to southern California, with their own demands for housing and transportation.

Consolidation with Los Angeles brought electric power, fire and police protection, and a guaranteed five-cent streetcar fare within city limits. But the crucial factor in the vote was the growing lack of water, for both human consumption as well as a necessity for fighting fires in the many wooden homes. Contrary to the impression given by the movie *Chinatown*, which sets these events in the 1930s, the water wars were well under way in the first decade of the twentieth century, when the city of Los Angeles had prohibited nonresidents from using wells fed by the Los Angeles River and began buying up land in the Owens Valley. In 1904 William Mulholland began construction of the aqueduct that would enable the city's great expansion. President Teddy Roosevelt supported the plan, and in June 1906 Congress approved the right of way. The aqueduct was completed in 1913, three years after Hollywood and Los Angeles consolidated, and the supply of fresh water it guaranteed induced towns all over the area to see their destiny as part of greater Los Angeles. In 1911, the Brooklyn-based Vitagraph film company opened a facility in the Franklin Hills to the east of Hollywood, and in 1912 Mack Sennett, a former actor for Griffith at Biograph, formed the Keystone Company, taking over the Bison lot on Allesandro Street in Edendale and beginning his series of great silent comedies with Fatty Arbuckle, Mabel Normand, Charlie Chaplin, and so many others.

As anyone who has seen these early films notices—whether the comedies of Sennett, the melodramas of Griffith, the westerns of Thomas Ince—while some scenes are shot on sets, many more are shot outside. And the outside was all over southern California. Downtown Los Angeles was often a setting, as were Venice and Santa Monica on the beach. Even though there were a few studios in Hollywood, most were on the periphery, toward Sunset Boulevard and below, where the rents were cheaper and there was less likelihood of interference by the Hollywood civic authorities, intent on protecting the purity of their community.

Others set up even farther away, like Balboa Films, which turned out some thousand movies in Long Beach between 1913 and 1918.

Even some years later, when Chaplin began making his own films instead of working for others, Hollywood was only rarely a setting. Intricately matching frames from Chaplin's early films with vintage photographs and modern settings, John Bengtson, building on the work of other locationologists and adding considerable material of his own, has traced the settings of a number of Chaplin's early shorts and features, which he has also done for Buster Keaton. One thing is clear: when in southern California, Chaplin spent most of his filmmaking time in Los Angeles, not Hollywood, with occasional forays to the beach in Venice, where Abbot Kinney had built a rival to Old Europe, complete with canals, pleasure domes, and stately hotels. Chaplin especially liked shooting in LA's Chinatown and in the Mexican area still present in the Plaza de Los Angeles and nearby Olvera Street, where Bengtson has fixed the setting of the great reunion of Charlie and Jackie Coogan in *The Kid* by the unique shape of the windows behind them.

Up until World War I, then, Hollywood, like the older city of Pasadena, which it often tried to emulate, was still a place for respectable retirement and second homes rather than premieres and movie stars. In 1908 Hollywood launched a Flower Parade with decorated vehicles like those in the Tournament of Roses begun in Pasadena in 1890. So far as the movie business was concerned, however, the commitment to southern California, let alone Los Angeles or Hollywood, was hardly yet very stable or enduring. But it was coming. A major commitment was made by D. W. Griffith, when he left Biograph in 1913 with his entire stock company after making *Judith of Bethulia* on an elaborate (and expensive) set in the San Fernando Valley. Yet most of the big companies—Biograph, Vitagraph, Famous Players–Lasky— still maintained offices in the New York area, where even in the heyday of the studio system the executive offices and finance still resided. Even Triangle, the combine of Griffith, Sennett, and Ince founded in Culver City in 1915, maintained offices in Fort Lee, New Jersey, into 1916, while Sennett continued to make his movies in Edendale. Essanay, another Chicago-based studio, had also in 1913 set up a California base for its popular westerns, starring Gilbert M. "Broncho Billy" Anderson. In 1914 Essanay hired Chaplin away from Sennett at Keystone for what turned out to be a year's worth of comedies, the first that Chaplin produced by himself. This all happened not in Hollywood or even Los Angeles, but in the small Bay Area town of Niles in northern California.

Whatever its lack of a recognizable center of operations, the movie business was nevertheless beginning to make its impact on American culture, not only through its films but through everything surrounding them as well. In the wake of the beginnings of the star system, when comedies could be advertised as featuring "Fatty and Mabel" or "Charlie" without any need to even hint at a plot, came the gossip columnists, once again originating more from afar than from southern California itself. Louella Parsons, who had been a scriptwriter for Essanay in Chicago, became perhaps the nation's first movie gossip columnist in 1914 for the Chicago *Record-Herald*, moving in 1918 to the New York *Telegraph* and in 1922 hired by William Randolph Hearst for his New York *American*, where she remained for the rest of her career, although living in Los Angeles. Chicago was also the home of *Photoplay*, one of the first and the most long-lived of fan magazines. Begun in 1911 with a producer-oriented focus on characters and plots, by 1915 it had changed into a vehicle for stories about rising and reigning movie stars, even to the extent in 1920 of giving its own Best Film award, which anticipated the Oscars by several years.

Staid old Los Angeles was also beginning to take notice. In the fall of 1914, the *Los Angeles Times* began a breezy weekly column called "Film Flams" written by Grace Kingsley and featuring more or less innocuous behind-the-scenes stories of films in production and other industry doings. Around the same time the *New York Times* introduced its own chronicle, "Written on the Screen." As yet, however, Hollywood or "Hollywood" still had not made its iconic appearance. An earlier story Kingsley wrote titled "Where Movies Are Hatched," with a subhead proclaiming "The Capital City of Movie Land," turns out to be about Universal Pictures in the San Fernando Valley. Hollywood is not even mentioned as an actual place, let alone as a term that everyone agrees means "the movies." In fact, until the 1920s the word "Hollywood" rarely if ever appears in the title of a film, even those films, usually comedies, that are about the movie business. The magic word was more often "photoplay" or "movies" or "film," as if movies, as in Buster Keaton's *Sherlock, Jr.* (1924), constituted a magical world with no actual existence on earth, where all the stars and all the stories existed timelessly together.

But the physical place called Hollywood could not hold off the expanding movie business forever, no matter how many prohibitive ordinances and hostile rooming house signs there might be. Movies meant money and the consolidation of Hollywood with Los Angeles, along with the increasing proximity of the two places by public transportation and, gradually, paved roads, started to bring money into Hollywood as well. Daeida Wilcox's legacy of civic self-control had weakened with her death in 1914. In that same year, one of the local millionaires living in the foothill mansion area above Hollywood Boulevard, perhaps more eccentric than most, an oddball among the otherwise conservative settlers, welcomed a film crew to his house.

The movie was *Tillie's Punctured Romance*, a farce based on a successful stage play called *Tillie's Nightmare* that starred Marie Dressler in New York. It was to be the first feature-length comedy ever filmed. With Dressler as Tillie, paired with Charlie Chaplin and Mabel Normand as two con artists after her money, and with ample help from Sennett's Keystone Kops, it was filmed on Venice Beach, in the Angeles Crest mountains, and around the lavish home of Dr. A. G. Schloesser at the corner of Franklin and Argyle Avenues in Hollywood. Released at the end of 1914, not long before *The Birth of a Nation*, *Tillie's Punctured Romance* was a movie beachhead deep in the heart of Hollywood. Until this point any image of Hollywood mansions on the screen tended to be from shots quickly stolen of the entrances or gates, after which the performers and the cameraman and director would beat a hasty retreat. But *Tillie's*, in addition to scenes with Chaplin and Normand on Hollywood Boulevard that included passing streetcars, featured whole sequences set outside and inside Dr. Schloesser's mansion, in the film supposedly the home of Tillie's uncle. Sometime during the shoot, a few photographs suggest, the proud doctor, wearing his signature top hat, posed smilingly with Mabel Normand and Marie Dressler.

Like Paul de Longpré, Schloesser represented European status and sophistication to the aspiring world of early Hollywood. Born in Chicago, Schloesser had made money in northern California mining before coming to Hollywood in 1899, where he made even more in real estate and loans. In 1906 he and his wife set out on a world tour that lasted four years and brought back his own modest (compared to Hearst's) share of European treasures. To house them he first built a Scottish castle. It sat a few blocks away from Beachwood Drive, which a decade and a half later became the entrance to the development called Hollywoodland.

Franklin and Prospect Avenue, the future Hollywood Boulevard, were the main sites of the early mansions of Hollywood.

Several of the most striking homes had an eclectic and exotic look, mixing foreign influences with the grandiosity of the upper-class East Coast mansions of Newport, Rhode Island. For de Longpré it was Moorish; for Horace Letts, another early Hollywood real estate magnate, it was the English half-timbered look; for the Bernheimer brothers, a pair of New York–based importers of cotton and Asian luxury goods, it was the Japanese style that they enshrined in Yamashiro, built between 1911 and 1914. For many years a fancy restaurant, Yamashiro still sits above the intersection of Hollywood and Highland, while just below it is the French Provincial private home that is now called the Magic Castle, built in 1909. Dr. Schloesser, for his part, first drew upon his wife's supposed ancestral castle near Inverness, Scotland, for the "Castle Glengarry" he built in 1908 (later sold to the actor S. I. Hayakawa), adding a few gothic elements from Castle Nuremberg. Three years later his model was the Rhenish Castle Rheinstein, "mixed with the Gothic halls of Baronial England," for a second "picturesque and stately castle home" on the other side of the street—where the scenes for *Tillie's* were filmed. On the announcement of these plans for what he called "Sans Souci" in 1911, the *Los Angeles Times* commented, "Hollywood, famous from coast to coast for its beautiful foothill homes, is soon to boast a new residential show place which bids fair to take rank among the tourist attractions of Southern California," and especially remarked the windows made of "art glass depicting the scenes of the days of chivalry."

Baum's Ozcot, built a year later, in contrast to these more fantastic creations, was, like many other early buildings, in essence an imitation of the East Coast Queen Anne–Eastlake style frame house, which in its turn was part of a revival (or misunderstanding) of earlier styles of the seventeenth and eighteenth centuries that was presided over by such prestigious New York firms as McKim, Mead, and White.[4] In some residential neighborhoods of Los Angeles, like Angeleno Heights near downtown and the area near the University of Southern California, these homes have been restored or at least prevented from decaying further. But the opening of Hollywood Boulevard to commercial buildings and the cutting down of the pepper trees planted by the Wilcoxes and their replacement with more photogenic "southern California" palm trees virtually doomed all but the hardiest survivors.

In the years before World War I, Ozcot, like Sans Souci, a few blocks away, partook of an urge to link the new Hollywood to a respectable, and prestigious, past. A desire to refashion midwestern American immigrants as belated descendants of the traditions of old California was also slowly gathering strength through adobe-style buildings and early Spanish Colonial Revival architecture, as well as through institutions like Fiesta parades and even sporadic efforts to restore the crumbling missions. But the more basic desire for West Coast respectability was, in the 1890s and early twentieth century, still in the direction of the East Coast, England, and continental Europe. Grand houses often resembled the splendor of what had been left behind in the East or Midwest, and it's hard to tell the difference between a great Los Angeles house of the 1890s and one from the same period depicted in a book like Margaret Keyes's *Nineteenth-Century Home Architecture of Iowa City.*

Giving his respectable imprimatur to *Tillie's Punctured Romance,* Dr. Schloesser, who a few years later during World War I changed his name to Castles because of a "hatred of all things Prussian," was the opening wedge in the door that beckoned filmmaking symbolically if not often in reality to Hollywood. The next major step, and one indicative of the wariness of the Hollywood city fathers and their respectable constituents about films and filmmaking, came in 1918, when Charlie Chaplin, for whom *Tillie's* was his first feature film role, opened his own studio on La Brea Avenue, just north of the southern boundary of Hollywood. Just as Sunset Boulevard was far enough away to allow some looseness, so Chaplin could be in Hollywood, if not quite of Hollywood.

"Hollywood" as a word that summoned up either Los Angeles or the movie business was still some years in the future, but things were starting to change. Not that studios were suddenly finding Hollywood the place to be. Aside from the rental of barns and taverns by the early filmmakers, the establishment of regular studios in the Hollywood area still lagged behind other parts of Los Angeles County. Many, then as now, were often elsewhere: MGM in Culver City, Universal in the San Fernando Valley, Warner Bros. in Burbank (after a short time on Sunset).

Following Chaplin's time at Essanay in Niles in 1915, he returned to Los Angeles to work for Mutual with his own studio, appropriately called Lone Star, in Colegrove, below Santa Monica Boulevard, later the site for much of Buster Keaton's feature filmmaking. At Mutual, Chaplin was more in charge of his own filmmaking than ever. But exclusive creative control as star, director, and producer was still another step away, as was a major move out of the periphery into Hollywood itself. There's no direct evidence that Dr. Schloesser worked to convince the Hollywood City Council to approve the building of new Chaplin studios in a citrus orchard on La Brea just north of a street now named after Paul de Longpré. But Schloesser's smiling acceptance of the filming of *Tillie's Punctured Romance* at his palatial home in 1914 may have helped, and, along with Chaplin's English accent, smoothed the way into Hollywood respectability as well. Chaplin himself tells the story in a little film he made in 1918 publicizing the move called *How to Make Movies*, to which he supplied a voiceover narration in the 1930s, reminiscing that the movie was made before the arrival in southern California of the "three horsemen of the apocalypse: oil, movies, and aeronautics." The film begins with a long shot of Chaplin and a man in flowing robes in front of a lemon orchard. There's a puff of smoke, and then in stop-motion the studio begins to rise, while we see in the distance the mansion where Chaplin and his brother Sydney would live. The architectural style of the studio, as a title says, is "Olde English Village." The Hollywood powers didn't want anything that looked like the ramshackle boxes that most studios were and, according to Chaplin, were placated by the facade. The *Los Angeles Times* reported: "As planned, [the buildings facing La Brea] offer no hint in their appearance of the purposes for which they are intended. The stages, dressing-rooms and other buildings will be well back from the street and out of the view of passersby." Passersby, perhaps, would not be enticed or upset, but the important move had nevertheless been made. Other studios had existed at the extremes of Hollywood or in neighboring towns. Here, for the first time, a major moviemaking enterprise was at the heart of Hollywood itself, and with the approval of its government and (most of) its residents.

Some lively opposition had in fact arisen, in which fears of outsiders raised by the bombing of the *Los Angeles Times* building in 1910 in the midst of a fierce unionization battle may have played a role. More tangible objections were raised by developers like Texas-born C. E. Toberman, nephew of a former Los Angeles mayor, who were worried that the presence of a studio so close to the palatial homes of Hollywood Boulevard would undermine their value. He argued instead for and later helped establish a separate Industrial District for the film business south of Santa Monica Boulevard. But ultimately the City Council voted 8 to 1 in favor of Chaplin's plan, after being assured that the studio would not be a distraction to students at nearby Hollywood High School. More significantly, they heard the testimony of the Merchants and Manufacturers Association about the importance of movie revenues to the fiscal health of Hollywood. One prominent banker commented even more strongly, "Mr. Chaplin has done more in the way of advertising Los Angeles than probably any other man." The studio would be physically in Hollywood, although Hollywood had still not yet become the name that would signify to the rest of the world the movie business in all its aspects, wherever it might actually be located. Hollywood snobbery about the "movies" was beginning to change, at least toward the rich and therefore respectable.[5]

Hollywood Becomes "Hollywood"

A sun-kissed miss said "don't be late."
That's why I can hardly wait,
Open up that Golden Gate,
California, here I come.
—B. G. DeSylva (1921)

Chaplin's swift rise, from a contract player at Keystone making $150 a week in 1913, then to the "lone star" at Mutual in 1916 at $10,000 a week (plus a $150,000 signing bonus), and finally on to owning his own studio little more than a year after that is only one of the most extreme examples of the tremendous leap made by the American movie business in the same years. Films like Griffith's *The Birth of a Nation* (1915) were showing that the movies had other, grander, aspirations than the one- and two-reelers of the nickelodeon days. Studios were expanding. Floods of wannabe actors and actresses, some with talent, many with only a desire for movie fame, were heading toward Los Angeles and Hollywood, swelling the population and enhancing the reputation of the growing city and the as yet small suburb as the Holy Grail of American ambition. Originally studios could set up anywhere in southern California and preferred to build in open unincorporated areas that would allow them to expand away from the prying eyes of local government. Now sets, like those in Chaplin's La Brea studio, were put on backlots to keep the growing crowds of gawkers at bay.

In the shorthand of film history, the French directors Louis Lumière and Georges Méliès—who were also both important early players in the American film industry—supposedly divide the artistic possibilities of cinema between them: Lumière with his live action scenes of ordinary life (trains arriving in stations, workers leaving a factory at the end of the day), Méliès with his fantasies of movie magic (a rocketship hitting the moon in the eye, magicians making things appear and disappear). Edison's early films tended to follow the Lumière side, while German film, until the 1920s the major national film industry, inclined more toward the artifice of Méliès, especially in such German expressionist classics as *The Golem*, *The Cabinet of Dr. Caligari*, and *Nosferatu*, with their dark, fatalistic visions.

Hollywood film in these polarized terms represented a third way, a mixture of realism of setting and fantasy of behavior, intense emotions combined with trademark logos on sets announcing the frankly constructed and branded nature of film reality. This intertwining of reality and fantasy in the movies lured audiences from all over America by an essentially American myth—the desire for self-creation, to be somebody, and to find a place in the new medium that was making that self-enhancement

possible. Half-serious, half-promotional ads summoned potential movie actors and actresses from around the country to come
and be recognized for who they really were, a heightened human
being called a movie star—or even to be disappointed, as in so
many early films, and discover there's no place like home.

For filmmakers coming out of the closed studios of the East,
where only occasional location shooting was possible, southern
California was a world of constantly available locations—urban
and rural, bucolic and arid, mountains and deserts—that could
easily stand in for most of the rest of the world. The capital cities
of Europe, as well as the established worlds of New York and
Chicago, could be explored or serve as backdrops for film. But
unlike Paris, London, or Berlin, Hollywood and the West were
not part of a mature urban setting with a long cultural history.
Instead, like American character itself, it was a raw new world,
filled with open space in which to build. By contrast with the storied
cities of the East and Europe, Los Angeles and Hollywood were
there to be created from the ground up, shaped and manipulated,
until they became every moviegoer's other world—cities of the
imagination. As the embryonic star system began to identify the
previously anonymous faces on the screen, "Hollywood" became a
catchall term for the mythic space where they all could be found.

Much more than other national cinemas, American film was
thus self-consciously aware of the influence of place on character, especially after the move to the West Coast. Geography became thematic and plot became destiny, especially of course for

the flood of westerns, but also as part of the atmosphere of shooting day-to-day in southern California locations, with their short
but intense history. For the immigrants who made up such a
large part of the early nickelodeon audiences, that openness was
an easy visual analogy to the lure of American freedom itself.

This self-conscious sense of place included as well a virtually
unique self-consciousness about the filmmaking process along
with a desire to put that process on film unparalleled in other
national film industries. *Tillie's Punctured Romance* offers an intriguing example of this desire to refer to the movies within the
movies. At one point, Chaplin and Normand, well dressed and
well fed on Dressler's money, go to a movie called *A Thief's Fate*.
There, according to the intertitle, they see "shady characters like
themselves on the screen." Here the movies self-mockingly and
self-importantly instruct their audiences on the moral significance of going to the movies. Of course such self-awareness exists almost exclusively in the realm of comedy. A melodramatic
storyteller like D. W. Griffith needs his audience to believe in a
film's transparency, that we are seeing something true, because
we are meant to be morally enlightened by it, without any wink-
ing smirks. A comedian like Mack Sennett takes a different ap-
proach. Emphasizing that we are watching a movie rather than
an immediate dramatic reality is part of a general mockery of all
authority, political as well as artistic. To allow a look behind the
scenes expresses an intimacy with the audience impossible for
the more histrionic stars of serious drama. Comedians—or pan-

tomimists, as they were often then called—like Normand, Arbuckle, and Chaplin look directly at us (that is, at the camera), creating a complicity with the audience like an aside on stage—"we're in this together"—that collapses the distance between performer and role, between us and them. The awareness of illusion is an essential part of the illusion. When Chaplin began to make features as a more "serious" director, he looked at the audience much more rarely: We are on his side, but not because he pleads directly for that identification.

The embedding of movies within movies also shows the need of entrepreneurial Hollywood filmmakers, unlike those in state-supported European industries, to engage in self-promotion and industry promotion. So many silent films deal with the journey of a character to become an actor. Usually it's someone from the Midwest, gone movie crazy, who comes out to make his or her fame and fortune. Like the midwestern migration to southern California itself that stretched from the 1880s into the 1920s, such stories emphasized the movies as the potential realization of dreams of psychic as much as physical health in the land of perpetual sun. The performers may have been stars, but they were also in some way normal and accessible, just as Hollywood presented itself as a heightened mirror of normal America. And when the films tell stories of people who come west to become stars, they aren't stage performers, who in fact were being lured by producers anxious to increase the respectability of the fledgling industry. Instead, they are just plain folks from the prairies.

faces show up in a film whose publicity poster features a large head emblazoned "Hollywood" swallowing up legions of young women, while in *Show People*, Douglas Fairbanks, William S. Hart, and John Gilbert have cameos, and Charlie Chaplin even stops the Davies character on the street and asks for her autograph![1]

By the early 1920s, then, with books, plays, and above all movies explicitly set in a movie world whose backstage life was already the object of journalistic and magazine celebration if not excessive scrutiny, "Hollywood" was on the way to becoming the blanket term that it is today. In the actual geographic Hollywood, the kind of moral control exerted by the old settlers over a comparatively small area was giving way to the big-town awareness of businessmen and bankers that the movies meant money. Hollywood was beginning to change. Paradoxically, despite Ordinance Ten and because of the coming of Prohibition to the entire country in 1919, the need for an isolated anti-alcohol utopia had vanished, and Hollywood the suburb already had its laxer areas. One of the great chroniclers of early Hollywood is Diana Serra Cary, who as Baby Peggy made 150 two-reeler comedies by the time she was three, many of them mocking the conventions of "grown-up" films. She writes in *The Hollywood Posse* of her father, a cowman who, like many others, came out during the winter to make money as an extra and stunt man. Even though Hollywood was a town with "more prohibitionists and millionaires than a Texas steer has ticks," Jack Montgomery, looking for a drink in dry Los Angeles, was told of a place called the Water-

Poster for the film *Hollywood* (1923), directed by James Cruze. Even though the
film is a comedy, the poster plays on recent scandals that characterize Hollywood
as a sink of iniquity, especially for young women.

hole off Sunset at Cahuenga, virtually around the corner from the barn where DeMille had made *The Squaw Man* a few years before.

Los Angeles, meanwhile, was heralding itself as "the best advertised city in the world," a beacon for visiting chambers of commerce from towns, particularly in the Midwest and West, that wanted to enhance their image. Even a delegation from Tombstone came to call in the early 1920s, forty years after the gunfight at the O.K. Corral, to see how that town might turn its bloody history into a tourist attraction. It was an era when advertising itself was being consolidated into an important American industry, and the merchandising skills developed during the early celebration of southern California and Los Angeles as the heartland of health and self-enhancement were a premium product.

A vital part of the equation that opened up the movie business to the nation and the world was a dawning awareness of the need to emphasize its artistic quality and professionalism. Instead of leaving the publicity entirely to the fan magazines and gossip columns, stars and moguls took center stage themselves, and their theme was respectability, social and aesthetic. In a vain corporate effort to retain the services of the previously almost anonymous D. W. Griffith, Biograph had placed an ad in the *New York Dramatic Mirror* in 1913 proclaiming him (with some exaggeration) as the great innovator of the close-up, cross-cutting, the fadeout, and other techniques of camera work and acting style. The movies were a significant artistic business, the poet

Vachel Lindsay agreed in *The Art of the Moving Picture* (1915), the first full-scale book of film criticism, praising Griffith, Ince, and others.

A year later the applied psychologist Hugo Munsterberg kicked off film theory with *The Photoplay: A Psychological Study*, and Rose Wilder Lane (the daughter of Laura Ingalls Wilder, later of *Little House on the Prairie* fame) ghosted a biography of Charlie Chaplin. In 1921 Mae Marsh, who had starred in *Birth of a Nation* and *Intolerance*, as well as some hundred other films, added the gloss of a professional craft with *Screen Acting*. Samuel Goldwyn, who raised Marsh's salary from the $35 a week she was making with Griffith to $2,500, was one of the early movie business's prime creators of prestige productions, based on successful plays and novels, and often starring European and New York theater performers. In an intriguing little book he published in 1923, the year the Hollywoodland sign went up, Goldwyn elaborated on his adventures so far in the film business and his impressions of various stars. He also refers to "Hollywood" generically, even when he is explicitly talking about studios in downtown Los Angeles and even faraway Long Beach. To complete the picture of intellectual and cultural importance, Terry Ramsaye, a film journalist and producer who had been in the business since 1915, published *A Million and One Nights: A History of the Motion Picture Through 1925*. Beginning with the visual language of Chinese pictographs and celebrating the contributions of Eadweard Muybridge, Thomas A. Edison, and early film technology, Ramsaye tells an elaborate story that included virtually every major inventor, producer, star, and director who contributed to the growth of the film business. By the late 1920s, then, film could boast that it was an art form, with an art theory, a professional craft, and now Ramsaye had given it a history.

The early 1920s therefore mark the moment when "Hollywood," with the newfound respectability as well as notoriety of the movies as an art and a business, begins to be the local habitation and name for all its aspects, no matter where they might be in reality. In the early 1920s, on their return from a European honeymoon tour, Douglas Fairbanks and Mary Pickford were interviewed by the *New York Times*, and Fairbanks insisted, "We do not live in Hollywood; we live at home." "Hollywood" had already become a heightened and, as far as Fairbanks was concerned, a negative idea. To get away from being so stereotyped, he and Pickford had moved to Pickfair in Beverly Hills, originally a ramshackle hunting lodge, then lavishly rebuilt over the years. In the teens, movie people still tended to live in apartments, hotels, or garden courts. Although she was a well-paid star for years, Mabel Normand didn't buy her first house until 1924. When the old Hollywood hostility toward movie people began to ease after *Birth of a Nation*, the Chaplin studio, and other movie enterprises brought a flow of money into the area, a certain number of stars, directors, and producers began buying homes in Hollywood. But even by the early 1920s, only some of the richest as yet had their own homes—and usually in other

parts of town. They preferred the more upper-class neighborhoods south of downtown Los Angeles like Chester Place in
West Adams. Fatty Arbuckle had a home there, previously owned
by Theda Bara (and later by the director Raoul Walsh), not more
than a block away from the mansion of Edward L. Doheny, one
of the pioneer oilmen of Los Angeles.[2]

The increasing focus on "Hollywood" as an emblematic center that held together a wide array of studios, stars, and all the
other paraphernalia of movie-making gave the film industry an
identity it didn't have when its operations were spread across the
country, or even divided between production in southern California, financial offices in New York, and distribution everywhere there was a theater. Like "Motown" or "Nashville" did
later in the music business, "Hollywood" merged a business with
a place (or at least a place name) to create a brand. In this history
of self-promotion, it's hard to disentangle what Hollywood
learned from California in general and Los Angeles in particular
from what the state and the city learned from the film business.
Al Jolson's hit song of 1924, "California, Here I Come," is an
intriguing mix of northern and southern California references.
"Open up that golden gate" directly invokes San Francisco Bay,
while "Sunkist" had been the trademark of the Southern California Fruit Exchange since 1893. After an almost exclusive preoccupation with the San Francisco area, first incited by the Gold
Rush and the 1906 earthquake, national attention now turned
southward to the idealized land depicted on the sides of orange

crates. There were other attractions as well. The Tournament of Roses had become a national spectacle since its beginnings in the 1890s, the Rose Bowl game began its long, prestigious career in 1916, and the annual production of *Ramona* in Hemet, with its romantic celebration of the continuity of old and new California, drew thousands of spectators beginning in 1923.

Meanwhile the formerly ragtag film business, lower class in origin and audience, dispensing cheap entertainment and low-brow antics, while often staying just a jump or two ahead of the sheriff or the Edison Trust, had learned how to consolidate, grow, and appeal to new middle-class viewers. The prestige of Griffith's highbrow filmmaking was one way to turn the movies into a serious art form, while Goldwyn's importation of famous theatrical stars and the adaptation of successful books and plays was another. But it was the growing sense of Hollywood as a special place that gave an aura not to just one filmmaker or one film but to the entire industry.

An even more decisive historical factor in the growing respectability of the film business, and a central reason for the preeminence of Hollywood that lasted from the teens into the 1960s, was war—war in Europe, that is, war that first stifled and then devastated the countries, especially Germany, France, and Italy, that had dominated and pioneered the young art form. Certainly there were innovators in America as well, but when World War I drastically cut down the number of films being made in Europe, a still-adolescent American film business had to grow up fast. Fortunately the patents of the oppressive Edison Trust had expired in 1913, and by 1918 the Edison appeal against an antitrust decision was dismissed by the Supreme Court, effectively ending whatever remaining power it and its members had over the making of motion pictures in the United States. In particular it was the German film industry, previously the biggest and most profitable in the world, that lost its predominance. By the 1920s more than 80 percent of global filmmaking originated in the United States, with German directors like Ernst Lubitsch and actors like Emil Jannings (winner of the first Oscar for best actor) seeking their fortune in Hollywood.

A significant part of selling the war to the American people, once the political decision had been made to intervene, was the presence of movie stars. In 1915, President Woodrow Wilson was treated to a special White House screening of *Birth of a Nation* by his former college classmate Thomas Dixon, who had written the play that the film was based on. According to Dixon, the impressed Wilson gave an immediate boost to the film's fortunes by calling it "like writing history with lightning." Whether Wilson actually said this or not, the need to encourage support for his war policy made the appeal to the movie industry a natural one, in order, as Wilson later wrote, "to give some measure of official recognition to an increasingly important factor in the development of our national life." William Brady, head of the National Association of the Motion Picture Industry, secretary of the Treasury William Gibbs McAdoo (Wilson's son-in-law), and the journalist George Creel, named by Wilson to run the Committee on Public Information, collaborated on bringing movie-star prestige to raise money for the war effort, while reciprocally bestowing cultural credit on the film industry for its war effort. Creel's 1920 book, *How We Advertised America*, mentions the movie-star support only in passing, but newspaper stories of the day tell of the huge crowds that turned out when the campaign for the Second Liberty Loan opened in Washington, D.C., with Fairbanks, Pickford, Chaplin, and Marie Dressler as speakers to encourage crowds to buy war bonds for the U.S. entry into the war in 1918.[3]

Wartime is always a fertile moment in which to define, directly and often simplistically, what is elemental in a nation's culture, a time when old icons are brandished as emblems of ancient unity and new ones created. Already deeply penetrating the national emotional life, movies and movie people gained the prestige of allying themselves with the country's political destiny as well. The subsequent postwar honeymoon tour of Europe by Fairbanks and Pickford, along with Chaplin's triumphant return visit to his English homeland, further showed how the movie business and its stars also had a deep international impact. What had started a scant decade before as a trickle of news about films and filmmakers was on the verge of becoming a deluge.

With money and patriotism also came the otherwise elusive social respectability. In 1925, eleven years after Grace Kingsley's more sporty "Film Flams" column in the *Los Angeles Times* came the dignified "Society of Cinemaland" column written by Isabel Stuyvesant and later Myra Nye, which surveyed the weddings, teas, and other social goings-on in the movie community with a heavy overlay of solemn decorum. Physically as well the movie-viewing experience was being transformed from its tacky origins as a screen in a converted storefront, then to a space resembling the legitimate theater, and finally to a grandly decorated picture-showing venue of unparalleled luxury and exoticism. By the early 1920s, pompous splendor was in the air. As Frances Marion recalled, "By 1924 everything in Hollywood was blown up to Brobdingnagian size, even the publicity on current productions."

A crucial figure in the construction of movie palaces and a creator of movie events that promoted "Hollywood" as the center of movie magic was the impresario Sid Grauman. Grauman had been in Alaska in the late 1890s, during the Klondike gold rush, where he grubstaked Wilson Mizner, the storied con man who with his architect brother Addison helped hype the Florida land boom of the early 1920s before being exposed as a swindler and fleeing for Los Angeles. Grauman, after building theaters in Alaska and northern California, came to Los Angeles and, like so many others, first focused on the downtown area, opening his Million Dollar Theater in 1918. But Hollywood beckoned, in the shape of the ubiquitous booster and developer C. E. Tober-man, for whom lavish movie palaces were part of his plan to make Hollywood Boulevard one of the great shopping streets of the world. In 1922 Grauman inaugurated the Egyptian, the first of his two magnificent Hollywood Boulevard theaters, and in 1927 the even grander Chinese Theatre, the same year as another Toberman project, the Hollywood Roosevelt Hotel, opened across the street.

Soon news photos of Grauman's premieres became a staple of entertainment news—the limousines, the red carpet, the klieg lights knifing through the sky, and the cement blocks where stars imprinted their hands and shoes and, not incidentally, engraved a few words of thanks to Grauman. The image of a Grauman premiere in a magazine or a newspaper created a focus by which the movie business could be understood, pulling together the many individual stars and their many films, wowing the Hollywood home folks as well as those far away, who heard or saw of it only second hand. Like the foundation of the Academy of Motion Picture Arts and Sciences in 1927, with Douglas Fairbanks as its first president, the Grauman premiere made an industry and a spectacle out of what before had only been a scattered group of competitive entrepreneurs. "Hollywood" was thus not so much a creation of the production of motion pictures as it was of their exhibition and publicity. To invoke the name "Hollywood"—like the 1923 hillside development that was to rise in Beachwood Canyon, or the 1925 city of Hollywood, Florida, promoted by the Mizners in the marshlands north of Miami—was to invest a project with a touch of the newest glamour, even though in the real geographic place few movies were made and few movie people lived.

■

Hollywood certainly needed a boost in the early 1920s, a glad hand and a round of applause, some upbeat news to push away darker thoughts. In the few years before the Hollywoodland sign went up, scandal had rocked the movie colony, and pulpit finger-pointers from around the country denounced the "cesspool of iniquity," to cite one of the milder attacks. The old prejudices against actors, it turned out, were only dormant. With each new scandal they came back in full force, while newspaper stories of wild parties fed the flames. As Frances Marion observed, the early years of Hollywood were filled with young people making more money than they had ever known before, and the social scene was no holds barred, fueled by the general hostility to Prohibition and in pursuit of everything that was roaring about the Twenties. First to make the news was the Fatty Arbuckle scandal in late 1921. Arbuckle and friends had gone up to party in San Francisco, always the getaway place for revelry compared to more staid Los Angeles. During the party, a starlet named Virginia Rappe was taken to the hospital in pain, and later died. Arbuckle was accused of rape and murder and, although acquitted in three trials, his career was effectively over, as theater owners around the country refused to show his films.

A few months later, William Desmond Taylor, an English-born director and three-time president of the Motion Picture Directors Association, was found murdered in his garden court home near downtown Los Angeles, shortly after being visited by Mabel Normand. In response, the studios quickly enlisted their writers to create a defense of the movie colony's morals, and there was a marked increase in churchgoing. As Terry Ramsaye remarks sardonically, "An atmosphere of sweet piety pervaded the shade of the palms and pepper trees of Vine street." Around the same time, the drug-shrouded death of the beautiful young Olive Thomas, the wife of Mary Pickford's brother Jack and the first actress to be called a flapper, as well as the death through morphine addiction of Wallace Reid, the handsome leading man in almost a hundred films, reinforced the feeling, especially among the conservative elements in the filmgoing audience, that there was more sin than transcendence in Hollywood. In 1924 Mabel Normand's chauffeur shot a young millionaire courting Normand, using her gun and in the presence of Normand herself and Edna Purviance, Chaplin's longtime leading lady. That incident, together with the Taylor murder, put Normand in the same censorious outer darkness as Arbuckle, even though she was never charged in either case. Finally, in late 1924 the film pioneer Thomas H. Ince was rushed from William Randolph Hearst's yacht and later died from what was diagnosed as heart disease exacerbated by acute indigestion. Rumors quickly had it that the cause was actually a bullet from the gun of Hearst who, jealous of Charlie Chaplin's attentions to his mistress Marion

Davies, had shot Ince in Davies's cabin, thinking it was Chaplin, or perhaps Ince was caught in the line of fire.

Whatever the truth of these stories, a sinister strain had definitely begun to appear in the glittering world, even though, as Ramsaye commented in 1926 (with no inkling in his metaphor of the anti-communism of decades later), "the truth about Hollywood was really a pink compromise between its homemade whitewash and the red glow of the sensational press." Young women, often considered by locals to be little better than prostitutes, had surged into the town looking for jobs and fun in this freer and easier world. But the Hollywood that was now synonymous with the movie business was beginning to run scared. Profits were being threatened when seven states and numerous towns and cities had their own censorship boards, let alone the censorship coming from foreign countries. In 1922 the Motion Picture Producers and Distributors Association (MPPDA) was formed to reassure audiences of the moral atmosphere both before and behind the camera. It was the first in Hollywood's attempts to meet criticism by what the movie business called self-regulation and liberal critics called self-censorship.

The role of the scandals in helping to make "Hollywood" a generic term was also significant. Until the early 1920s most newspapers around the country merely used the word as a place name, notable, if at all, for its fine homes and lush gardens à la Paul de Longpré. But just as the growing cultural significance of the film business impelled out-of-town newspapers to begin their own gossip columns to satisfy the curiosity of their readers, the rash of scandals focused a more malevolent sort of attention. In a desperate effort to defend the old Hollywood against the new, for example, a writer in the *Christian Science Monitor* in 1922, under the headline "Be Fair to Hollywood," chastised the Illinois town of Hollywood that wanted its name changed in response to the scandals, praised Hollywood's natural beauty, and concluded that "Hollywood's only failings have been thrust upon her by Broadway." So much for the film business's efforts to buy respectability from the legitimate stage!

From the very start of its penetration into the national psyche as a blanket term for the movie business, "Hollywood" therefore had a Jekyll and Hyde character. Not that, on the Hyde side, Hollywood was the only scandalous part of Los Angeles in the 1920s. The bribery and corruption behind the Teapot Dome oil leases were gradually being revealed, and suspicion was especially directed against Edward L. Doheny, Arbuckle's erstwhile neighbor on Adams Boulevard. But somehow Hollywood scandal seemed more pervasive and more intriguing than scandal in other areas of American life, perhaps because Arbuckle—like Normand, Chaplin, Lloyd, Keaton, Laurel and Hardy, and others— had as comedians a patina of innocence as part of their appeal. When scandal touched any of them, the disillusionment among their audiences was therefore more profound. So the fundamentalist moralism, like an avatar of old Hollywood lurking in the wings, came back to center stage, whether justified or not, ready to pounce on the new national scapegoat. In Hollywood itself the effort to exorcise the bad publicity took a more stately form, by emphasizing the local piety of the annual Pilgrimage Play, Hollywood's own Oberammergau, which had begun in 1919, and the Hollywood Bowl Easter Sunrise services, a tradition since 1921.

■

When the planning began for the development of Hollywoodland and the mammoth sign that would announce it, "Hollywood" thus was coming to mean something decidedly different from the town that the Wilcoxes had founded and developers like H. J. Whitley had expanded upon in the early years of the twentieth century. When we look back on early 1920s Hollywood, with its mixture of grand aspirations to respectability and ominous scandal, the increasing grandiosity of movie palaces, as well as the expanding self-promotion of the movie business, seem to be efforts to compensate for the shame and bad box office of the scandals, celebrating Hollywood's artistic and social ambitions instead of its gossip-fed private life.

If anyone could be called the founder of this next phase of Hollywood, it would possibly be a combination of the longtime developer Toberman, who also had a hand in the Hollywood Bowl, and the impresario Grauman, whose combined efforts brought the name to a national prominence it never had before. Also in the running would be Harrison Gray Otis (like Daeida Wilcox, born in Ohio), the founder of the modern *Los Angeles*

Times, and his son-in-law Harry Chandler, who ran the newspaper from 1917 to 1944, and whose first job as a sickly seventeen-year-old transplant had been picking oranges in the orchards of Hollywood. Long committed to boosting the region and not loath to benefit from it, the *Times* under Otis and Chandler had supported the building of the Los Angeles Aqueduct in the first decade of the twentieth century and continued to trumpet the virtues of the region until the Great Depression beginning in the late 1920s introduced a few mild notes of caution about unlimited growth.

But for the early 1920s especially, the *Times* was cheerleader, organizer, and participant in the expansion of Los Angeles, and its owners were not shy about profiting from it. Historians have counted some fourteen hundred developments begun in the Los Angeles area between 1922 and 1924, and 1923 was the peak year for building permits, with some sixty-three thousand being issued, worth $200 million (equivalent to about $2.5 billion today). The Florida housing bubble had not yet burst; the sons of Frederick Law Olmsted, the prestigious designer of Central Park, were carrying on their father's city-planning work on the Palos Verdes Peninsula; and the automobile, with its ability to access potential neighborhoods far beyond the reach of public transportation, was newly available to middle-class wallets. To top it off, a *Times* headline in August 1923 proclaimed "Los Angeles Officially Declared America's Finest Place to Live," certified by, of all people, the New York City Weather Bureau forecaster.

The symbiosis of real estate, advertising, and the sense of a special place enhanced by a relentless boosterism was hardly new to southern California. Advertising was the intermediary between the raw land and the more abstract idea of what would happen to the buyer after he or she was settled. Here especially the vision of a better self could be anchored in the land. Like the boosters, the film producers were also selling possibility and potential, manufacturing charisma in their stars and projecting fantasy in their stories. Building on the dreams of gold and health that animated so many of the early settlers, the movie business promised an even more durable, because less tangible, personal enrichment. "California, here I come."

Architecturally, the Queen Anne and shingle-style mansions of the past decades were giving way to a more regionally appropriate Spanish Colonial Revival style, and in the process Los Angeles stopped being an often slavish imitation of an East Coast or midwestern city. For less wealthy buyers came the democratic idea of the compact bungalow style, a house with a modest garden, influenced by the Craftsman style of the Pasadena-based architects Charles and Henry Greene (born in Cincinnati), that were filling up the previously empty streets that stretched south toward the oil fields of Wilshire and bordered the eastern limit of Hollywood in the direction of Los Angeles. The more adventurous among the wealthy of the 1920s and 1930s meanwhile commissioned architects like Frank Lloyd Wright, his son Lloyd, Richard Neutra, and Rudolf Schindler, who had arrived in southern California to build newly reimagined domestic and family homes in the unconditioned space. And to cap it off, Hollywood had become a household name. What better time to start a development called "Hollywoodland"?

The site of the new development in upper Beachwood Canyon was an old ranch, about a mile square, where in 1916 the natural amphitheater at the top of the canyon had hosted an epic production of *Julius Caesar*, with Tyrone Power (Sr.) as Brutus, William Farnum as Marc Antony, five hundred dancing girls, elephants, camels, and a supporting cast of five thousand. As construction began, roads were paved and streetlights installed, stripping the canyons and ravines of almost all vegetation to prepare the land for the houses to follow. Harrison Gray Otis and Harry Chandler were two of the principal backers of Hollywoodland, John D. Roche the main publicist, and Tracy E. Shoults the head of the Hollywoodland Realty Company. In addition to work beginning on constructing roads, grading plots, and putting in utility services, Theodore Payne, the pioneering southern California botanist and horticulturalist, was hired to sow tons of wildflower seeds and plant native shrubs. Opening in the spring of 1923, by September $1.25 million in home sites had been sold in Hollywoodland (equivalent to almost $16 million today). At least according to the *Times*, which of course had a special interest in keeping the momentum going, sales continued to grow until almost all parcels were gone.

By the time development began in Hollywoodland, the hills

Publicity photo for the Hollywoodland groundbreaking, complete with plow, mules, and surveyors (Courtesy of hollywoodpictures.com)

above Hollywood and the frost-free belt were starting to be filled in. Houses had already been built in the lower reaches of some of the neighboring hillsides and a few blocks up Beachwood Drive itself, thanks to the Albert H. Beach Company, which had also been instrumental in developing the Theosophist community of Krotona. Even now, these neighborhoods are filled with the tidily maintained bungalows and Spanish Colonial Revival homes of the numerous migrants to Los Angeles who don't have stars on Hollywood Boulevard. In reaction against the European and East Coast models followed in the late nineteenth and early twentieth centuries, a new architectural energy was in the air, with a special emphasis—among the revivalists as well as the avant-garde—on the shifting relationship between indoors and outdoors and the need to harmonize a house with its setting instead of imposing itself upon it. Modernists like Neutra and Schindler had a general hostility to the invocation of past styles, but in the big developments eclecticism abounded, especially leaning toward Mission and Spanish Colonial Revival, with their sentimental relation to the land. As the architectural historian Merry Ovnick has commented, Mission Revival in fact was the first indigenous southern California style, "well-watered by romantic notions, but native none the less." Styles in Hollywoodland were more various, although generally restricted to French Normandy, Tudor English, Mediterranean, and Spanish, with Spanish Colonial favored.

To Harry Chandler goes a large part of the credit for the creation of the sign. The 1920s "Straight Ahead for Southern California" promotional campaign of the *Times* had been insistent on signs as emblems of the new developments, and a road sign even began appearing in the newspaper's logo in 1921. Marketing and marking the landscape had begun even earlier, with the founding of the Auto Club of Southern California in 1900, a few years before there was a national organization. Billboards too were a tradition in the otherwise unmarked American landscape. A billboard lobbying group had been established in 1872, organized nationally in 1891, and already in 1909 there had been a failed suit to ban billboards in California, which gave way to the extensive use of billboards during the 1910 gubernatorial campaign.

In Los Angeles there had been continuing controversy over billboards since the late 1800s, which included constitutional challenges to city ordinances, stories of eyesores, accidents, and crimes committed because of billboard placement. Advocates of the "City Beautiful" were especially angry at the proliferation. One of the chief offenders against what one defender called "an esthetic town" was H. G. Wilshire, the namesake of Wilshire Boulevard, who was a unique combination of militant socialist, voracious land developer, and billboard advocate. He was fondly referred to in his hometown newspaper as "Bughouse Wilshire." Finally, after years of complaints on both sides, a City Council that the *Los Angeles Times* referred to as "acrobatic" passed a "wishy-washy" ordinance in 1917. The *Times* story, which was clearly on the side of the anti-billboard faction, highlighted in a box—presumably for ridicule—a remarkable statement by a member of the Echo Park Civic Association as an example of the "profuse persiflage" mustered by the billboard supporters:

> The billboards revivify the landscape and take the minds of our tourist hosts from the dull brown hills that the boards hide. They are educational, informing the travelers of our beauty spots, and otherwise giving them instructions of merit.

By the time Hollywoodland was in the planning stages, then, billboards were a normal part of the Los Angeles landscape.

Starlets in a steamshovel. Were they lent by Mack Sennett for Hollywoodland publicity? The back of the sign is visible at the bottom. (Courtesy of
hollywoodpictures.com)

Around the country, the jingling roadside Burma Shave signs
first began appearing in 1925, but few of these roadside entice-
ments could match the ostentation of the Hollywoodland sign.

John D. Roche, the publicist and later supervisor of the sign's
building, had penciled in "Hollywoodland" in a preliminary
drawing, and Harry Chandler liked the idea. "I want people to be
able to see it from Wilshire," said Chandler. What he no doubt
meant was that he wanted it to be seen by someone in a car, driving along what was being dubbed by boosters as the "boulevard

to the sea." The bungalow housing of the previous decade was essentially lower middle class, dependent on public transportation, whereas the new hillside developments with their pricier homes depended essentially on the car. Wilshire Boulevard was then still in parts a dirt road, although it was soon developed into the "Miracle Mile" between La Brea and Fairfax, as perhaps the first commercial district in the world to be designed for automobile traffic, with timed traffic lights, parking lots supplied by merchants, and ostentatious signage.[4]

Although Woodrow Wilson had commented that the sight of rich people driving in the expensive early automobiles was the prime cause of the "socialistic" atmosphere in the United States, by the 1920s Henry Ford's inexpensive Model T, folksily known as the "Tin Lizzy," together with the arrival of installment buying, made car ownership a middle-class privilege and necessity. The expansion of car ownership was a vital element in the movement of real estate development to the Hollywood Hills as well as for the creation of the Hollywoodland sign. In 1912 California had 76,669 registered cars. By 1920, the number was 604,187. By 1925, Los Angeles had the "highest per capita car ownership in the world." During the first quarter of the twentieth century, ten miles of American concrete highways had ballooned into twenty thousand, and state legislatures haggled over new taxes and expenditures to meet the growing demand for good roads. The popularity of the enclosed sedan was on the horizon, but most of these cars were open, and a great proportion of those Los Angeles car owners spent their weekend traveling from one part of the city to another, looking at the new developments, taking in the sights, and being dazzled with the growth of signs. In Hollywood and elsewhere streets originally designed for other kinds of traffic were being widened for the new surge of car ownership. An area that had ten miles of streets paved in 1926 had two hundred miles in 1927.

Not everyone was happy with the change. As Frances Marion remarked, on returning to Los Angeles and Hollywood in the early 1920s, "the heavenly scent of orange blossoms [was gone] and in its place was the stifling odor of gasoline," accompanying "the latest fad in architectural nightmares: stores and cafes in the shape of windmills, huge wieners, bulldogs, jails, and brown derbies." In the context of all these eye-grabbing objects in the landscape, the Hollywoodland sign was only the most grandiose. As the Auto Club's brand-new Spanish Colonial Revival headquarters at the corner of Adams and Figueroa indicated, the railroad-assisted real estate boom of the 1880s had decisively been surpassed. Now it was the car that carried tourists and downtowners past the billboards that helped turn them into landowners. The Auto Club of Southern California joined the boostery All Year Club to keep the tourist lures coming. As one of many efforts to turn sightseers into buyers, Harry Chandler, a director of the Auto Club since 1913, formed a club committee with Herbert Hoover and Luther Burbank to promote the restoration of the old Spanish missions.

Hollywoodland, then, would not have existed without the car. The development had the public stairways that were built in an older Los Angeles—as, for example, in the rugged areas near Mack Sennett's Allesandro Keystone studio—which allowed people who depended on public transportation to climb to their hillside homes after getting off the streetcar. But the stairways in Hollywoodland, however beautiful, sculpted, and planted with flowers, what were they for? Right at the gates of the development, along with a small complex of stores, was a gas station, and few of the new inhabitants would be traipsing up and down the stairs for their marketing. Walking hardly fit the image of luxurious leisure publicized by the ads. Many of the early articles about Hollywoodland stressed the care taken with grading the roads, one of them describing a motor trip over shale to the Hollywoodland sign itself, featuring a car with the superior ability to traverse slippery ground.

The stairways, like the styles of the homes, were less functional than picturesque, reminiscent of old Hollywood and old California, and old England, and old France, and old Italy—all-purpose nostalgia meant to soothe the modern homeowner. The heart of the package was modern convenience with old world charm, or, as one ad said, modern homes set among the "world-old" canyons. It was similar to but not quite the same as George F. Babbitt's "Cheerful Modern Houses for Medium Incomes." A bit more costly and certainly more exclusive than that, along with a guarantee that the neighborhood wouldn't change for fifty years. This claim might have been an allusion to a recent California Supreme Court ruling that upheld the legality of restrictive covenants on occupancy that had begun with a case from Los Angeles. Part of the "Straight Ahead for Southern California" campaign had been the boast, supported by the United States Chamber of Commerce, that the Los Angeles area was the "white spot" of American prosperity, and the racial implications of the metaphor were scarcely submerged. The 1920 lease on the land where my own home was built in 1927 stipulates "That none of the real estate described herein nor any portion thereof, nor any building on the same, shall be sold, conveyed, leased or rented to, or occupied by other than of the Caucasian Race." In contrast to what the demographer John H. M. Laslett describes as an era of "racial mixing and racial tolerance" between 1880 and 1920, postwar boosterism had created a kind of "anglo apartheid" that lasted for a time even after restrictive covenants were overthrown by the U.S. Supreme Court in the wake of World War II, coincidentally enough in a movement started by another Los Angeles case.

Where did Roche's idea for the sign come from? Billboards give one clue. Another comes from early photographs that show on a nearby hill an "H," for Hollywood High (founded in 1903). Made of wood, with tin sheets later nailed on, this "H" was constructed in 1922, a year before the Hollywoodland sign, on the slopes of a peak in the Hollywood Hills west of the Cahuenga Pass known as the Camel's Back. It was an early example of a

The entrance to Hollywoodland in 1924, with the stone gates in the foreground
and the Hollywoodland Realty Company office to the right of center
(Courtesy of hollywoodpictures.com)

collegiate-inspired American tradition of imprinting school letters on the land that began in California with the "C" in the hills
above Berkeley in 1905, and quickly spread across the country.

The lighting of the sign by 4,000 twenty-watt bulbs, another
crucial element in its ability to be seen at a distance, may have
been influenced by the ubiquitous wooden derricks in Los Angeles, otherwise an eyesore, that had for some time been rigged out
with electric lights as part of publicity for the oil industry. Elec-
tricity and, not much later, neon and searchlights were quickly
becoming some of the necessities of American advertising, especially when it came to the movies. But the most direct influence

was more likely the lavish premieres organized by Sid Grauman at his Egyptian and Chinese theaters, which were already part of the growing "Hollywood" image as a prime entertainment center. As early as 1915 Grauman was being celebrated for his elaborate use of a mass of electric searchlights to publicize his previous theaters and their attractions. His most elaborate attentions were given to what he called prologues, which were lavishly produced live introductions to long-running films at the Egyptian and later the Chinese that were thematically related to whatever film was to come. Early on, Grauman had scored a coup by having the actual stars of the films be part of the show as well, either as performers or in the audience, for the amazement of those who crowded the streets outside to wait for their appearance. The Egyptian had opened with Douglas Fairbanks in *Robin Hood* in 1922 for a six-month run, while the first film at the Chinese was Cecil B. DeMille's *King of Kings*.

All the lighting for the premieres was designed and the equipment invented by Otto K. Olesen, who had the lights and generators specially built. Born in Denmark, Olesen arrived in Hollywood in 1912 and first made a reputation designing lights for enclosed studio sets that were used on those not so rare days without sun. In 1918, armed with two war surplus searchlights he ventured into other kinds of illumination, first setting up a grand premiere for a new car dealership—another one of those intriguing Los Angeles interconnections between advertising, automobiles, and new technology. Fresh from his own interest in spectacle, Sid Grauman took notice and hired Olesen to do the premiere of *Robin Hood*. As other impresarios and promoters became aware of his work for Grauman, Olesen took his equipment to some fifty events a year over the whole state of California, even including a full-scale illumination of the Golden Gate Bridge for its opening in 1937. His lights also heralded the Academy Award presentation for many years. Among his own favorite projects were the *King of Kings* premiere that opened the Chinese, and the 1930 opening of *Hell's Angels*, which featured two hundred searchlights, huge advertising balloons, and smoke screens against which the name of the film was projected. Appropriately enough, on the Hollywoodland brochure for 1927 there is an image of an Olesen-lit Hollywood Boulevard, with the shafts of searchlights cutting through the night sky.

What about the name of the development? We have already seen why "Hollywood" was considered now to be the major lure. But why "land"? As Sinclair Lewis parodied in *Babbitt*, the need for a catchy name for new real estate developments was an essential part of the draw. "Restful Acres" or "Noble Heights" would pull in buyers who were looking for a style of self-definition as much as they were for bricks, mortar, and a family room. Although "land" as a suffix has become shopworn by now, more suitable to amusement parks than to neighborhoods, it was comparatively new then and may have been added in 1923 as a tribute to "Wonderland," Lewis Carroll's magical world, or, even closer in time, to "Neverland." J. M. Barrie's *Peter Pan* had been

a play in 1904, a novel in 1911, and in 1921 Paramount and Famous Players–Lasky announced a film, finally released in 1924.
But whatever the reminiscence of Carroll and Barrie, the suffix
had established itself as referring to a special dreamlike place,
like Victor Herbert's *Babes in Toyland* (1903), a general feel-good
association that Disneyland and so many other "lands" would
capitalize on in the years to come.[5]

"Hollywoodland," the sign proclaimed. Scaled by Roche for
the perspective from Wilshire Boulevard, the letters were forty-
five feet high, not in the sinuous Art Nouveau lettering of a past
world, but in a blocky sans serif typeface dictated in part by the
materials used and in part by the effort to project a contemporary image, Roche's own background as a typographer and
printer no doubt playing a role. Each letter was anchored on
telephone poles brought to the site by mules, driven into the
earth by Mexican laborers, and completed in sixty days at a cost
of $21,000 (more than $250,000 today). The skewed arrangement of the letters generally faced east, away from the ocean and
toward the land, where the buyers would presumably be coming
from. According to Roche, the four thousand bulbs came later,
inserted every eight inches, and the sign had four stages of illumination at night: "HOLLY," "WOOD," "LAND," "HOLLYWOOD-
LAND." To replace burned-out bulbs, a man named Albert Kothe
was hired, who lived in a house nearby and went about his job by
lowering himself in a bosun's chair from the top of the letters.[6]

The nicely flattened mesa-like top of the almost seventeen-

Hollywoodland sign illuminated (Courtesy of hollywoodpictures.com)

hundred-foot summit that so well frames the sign was owed to Mack Sennett, a minor investor in the Hollywoodland project, who had major ideas of his own for a house. Thinking to have an enormous mansion above the sign befitting the King of Comedy, Sennett bought 304 acres on the summit. As he writes in his autobiography, he wanted this highly visible place so that "everybody who goes by will point and say, 'That's where Mack Sennett lives.'" Perched on the ridge between the Los Angeles Basin and the San Fernando Valley, Sennett's mansion was designed to be visible from both sides, and a few years later he built studios in the valley that came to be called Studio City.

Because there was no road access to the future site, Sennett's mother took charge of the project:

> She put on an old straw hat and spent every day bossing the road gangs and steam rollers up and down that mountain. She got a road to the top, too, but we found the top wasn't flat. This meant slicing off sixty-nine feet of hard rock and shale to get a level of about four acres. But Mother did it.[7]

According to his often fanciful autobiography, Sennett and his mother then bought five hundred hogs to control all the snakes on the house site. The hogs later ran wild into the hills, whether before or after they had eaten the snakes is unclear. Since no one to this day has mentioned feral packs of pigs in the Hollywood Hills, this may be another exaggeration. Or perhaps there were no sows.

Filled with optimism, Sennett then hired an architect named John DeLario, who designed many of the homes in Hollywood-land, including a Norman-French château model home, a hilltop mansion called Castillo del Lago (later painted in red and yellow stripes by Madonna) and the Hollywoodland Realty Company office itself. The proposed house included a suite for Sennett's mother, guest rooms, mineral springs, a theater, tennis courts, bridle paths, and a miniature golf course—one of the great fads of the 1920s. A drawing of the grand mansion with a typed description can be seen in the Mack Sennett Collection in the Margaret Herrick Library of the Motion Picture Academy. But Sennett never broke ground on the peak he called Mount Sennett. The land was basically too inaccessible, even after his mother had supervised the grading and let loose the hogs. After briefly considering the installation of an elevator to the house, perhaps in imitation of the elevator to the Southwest Museum, Los Angeles's first, Sennett put the project on hold.

Still the appeal of being on the heights attracted more than just a Hollywood mogul, and the promotional material for Hollywoodland generally focused on people who lived on the flats in downtown Los Angeles, although they could appeal to anyone wanting to escape the urban world, "gasoline fumes," and crowds. Virtually every week through 1924 a big display ad appeared in the *Los Angeles Times*, adorned with drawings depicting the pleasures of Hollywoodland, with copy that had an increasingly alarmist tinge. The earliest featured palatial homes and men and women on horses with prospects of the hills, and, for contrast, the crowded streets of the city, "the maelstrom of human existence," versus Hollywoodland, "the Supreme Achievement in Community Building." The contrast wasn't that much of an exaggeration, since that same year a study had described Los Angeles as having "the most fouled-up and congested downtown streets of any city in the world." Still another ad featured a couple in a snappy roadster entering the Hollywoodland gates, leaving behind them like a bad dream those crowded streets and entering the vertical prestige of the hills, with a barely submerged allusion to the ladder of success. Urbanization was the enemy, and no reader could miss the intended contrast between the sunny, clear air of the new development and the crowded streets and dank tenements of the immigrant East Coast.

Total retreat of the sort that animated the early founders of Hollywood might no longer be possible, but respite and daily replenishing could be found on the Hollywoodland island for anyone with the wherewithal and racial profile to buy in. Hillside development was the antidote to the flatlands, and Swiss developers and surveyors came to get pointers on how to build on extreme slopes. Hollywoodland, the copy proclaimed, was "the Kingdom of Joy and Health," where you can leave behind the city "in order to *protect your family* and *insure their happiness*" with a house "above the smoke, fog and impure atmospheric conditions." Later the appeal expanded to stress how a move to Hollywoodland especially protected children from the dangers of the city—"Give the Kiddies a Chance!"—keep them away from "dangerous street corners." Buy a house in Hollywoodland, "For your family's sake."

But for all the invocation of the name, what did Hollywoodland mean in terms of Hollywood? Hollywood was a selling point, but which Hollywood was it? In the early newspaper ads, which dry up in 1925, there is no mention of the proximity to what was increasingly being referred to as the "movie capital" or "the movie colony." These were homes for the upper middle class, and with the shadow of scandal still in the air, the connection to the Hollywood that existed before "Hollywood" was stronger than to the contemporary movie community. True, the cover of that 1927 brochure features a blocks-long array of searchlights along Hollywood Boulevard, and the development advertises itself as "Five Minutes from Hollywood's Great White Way." But if there is any effort to bask in the movie aura, it is at a safe distance. When the Chinese Theatre does make a cameo appearance, it's as only one of a large number of neighborhood attractions along Hollywood Boulevard.

In the brochure's allusions to the prominent residents of Hollywoodland, there is not one movie star to entice new buyers, and the only one with even the hint of a connection to the media is a Hearst humor columnist named Kenneth C. Beaton. In fact, if the brochure has any real argument to make about Hollywoodland, it is to stress the quickness of the growth of vegetation in the previously bare hills, with several before-and-after pictures of houses and plantings, showing how the landscape grows up around the house and the house becomes integrated with the landscape, not separate from it. To complement this image of the affinity of the Hollywoodland home with a friendly, embracing nature, there is also a stress on the closeness to Griffith Park's bridle paths.

Historians of domestic architecture have long argued over which came first, houses or sets, Hollywood real estate make-believe or "Hollywood" movie make-believe. It's hard to establish priority, especially in an area where exotic sets were a normal sight, and where the landscape and climate are so hospitable to a sense of play. From the late nineteenth century onward, real estate in southern California was as much a fantasy as a response to environment, since the environment itself contained a large chunk of fantasy. It produced a grab bag of themes and motifs from the ages eclectically thrown together to create different images of architectural wonderment that were less authentic than meta-authentic, connected to a sense of place not by fidelity so much as by eccentricity. In the 1927 brochure for Hollywoodland, the advertising urge to bring together artifice and nature seems to have shifted the balance more toward nature than toward the glitter of Hollywood artifice. Grand plans were already being threatened by the oncoming Depression. Properties were getting harder to sell, and the much-heralded eastward continuation of Mulholland Drive into the hills above Hollywoodland as the Mulholland Highway remained for the most part unpaved, a dirt road to this day.

THREE

Hooray for Hollywood

The real story of Hollywood is a tragedy in a gilt jacket.
—MOLLIE MERRICK (1932)

Hooray for Hollywood, that screwy, ballyhooey Hollywood!
—JOHNNY MERCER (1936)

With the establishment of Hollywoodland, the many Hollywoods start to find a focus and a generally accepted meaning. First, there was Hollywood, the former village turned suburb turned part of Los Angeles—a specific place with geographic boundaries, constantly changing and contested. Then there was Hollywood as a generally accepted name for the homeland of the American movie industry, like Fleet Street in London for newspapers or Wall Street in New York for finance, a shorthand for the stars and the films. Then, allied to that sense of physical place was yet another Hollywood, a more or less intangible place on earth or in the atmosphere above it, to which aspirants to fame could come and be recognized. And finally, like a barely hidden prize in a candy box was the Hollywood in the Hollywoodland sign that would come to represent all of them—and a good part of the lure of Los Angeles itself. But it would be several decades before any sizable group of people in the area, the nation, or the world believed that a hillside sign was the palpable embodiment of that meaning.

The Depression that for several years halted the rampaging development in southern California, as developers went out of business and banks pulled back from residential financing, was only a few years in the future. So far in the mid-1920s, however, real estate energy was still in the air, and people from around the country came to southern California to buy and to sell. The virtually weekly Hollywoodland ads drop out of the *Los Angeles Times* by 1925, but other developers were undaunted. As old photographs show, just to the east of Hollywoodland a new development named Tryon Ridge posted its own set of giant white letters. Still another post-Hollywoodland development is more worth noting: Outpost Canyon, several wrinkles in the Hollywood Hills and Santa Monica Mountains west of Hollywoodland. Like Hollywoodland, Outpost has intriguing connections to the *Times*. Originally owned by the Californio Don Tomás Urquidez, who built the first adobe in Hollywood there in 1853, it was later bought by Harrison Gray Otis for a rustic clubhouse he called "The Outpost." Around 1914 the developer C. E. Toberman bought up some of the land, later sold it to the producer Jesse Lasky, and then in the 1920s, with the decisive success of the new "hill-side development" of Hollywoodland in front of him, bought a portion of the land back from Lasky and began developing it.

These were the same years in which Toberman, in partnership with Sid Grauman, was also developing the Egyptian and Chinese theaters. Outpost was therefore in many ways closer to Hollywood as an idea than was Hollywoodland, where the actual Hollywood seems to have been kept at a discreet distance in order to entice more respectable buyers. Dolores Del Rio is featured in the Outpost brochure as a committed home builder; in an early photo the Outpost sign is visible just beyond one of the architectural curlicues of the Chinese Theatre; and a few years later Outpost publicity noted that Bela Lugosi had recently bought an innovative steel-frame and concrete-slab house aimed to protect its owner from wildfires and termites. Instead of electric bulbs, the Outpost sign, striving to be at least as prominent as the Hollywoodland sign, featured red neon. It was a cutting-edge technology for advertising that Los Angeles had been the first city in the country to take advantage of just a few years before. In 1923 a Packard dealer named Earle C. Anthony, who as a teenage hobbyist in 1897 had built his own car, bought two blue and orange neon signs from France for his showroom at Olympic Boulevard and Hope Street. Along with the neon, Toberman topped off the homebuying lure with a characteristic Hollywood juxtaposition of the technological future and the sentimental past: Prospective landowners were invited to a presentation in the canyon next to a six-hundred-year-old sycamore that had been supposedly used as a hanging tree for the cattle rustlers of Hollywood's early history.

But the Depression nevertheless marked a distinct lull in the expansion of Los Angeles. Although snippets of land were still being added, the first grand era of city annexation and consolidation was over. The biggest single jump in surface area had come with the annexation of the San Fernando Valley in 1915, and population kept pace. In 1920 Los Angeles became the largest city in California, and then in 1930, four times as populated as it had been in 1910, it became the fifth largest in the country.

The migration from the Midwest slowed to a trickle, but for a time at least the fortunes of both Hollywood and Los Angeles were high. The studios, which had begun as haphazard business endeavors a decade or so earlier, had started to consolidate, absorbing their weaker competitors, and organizing themselves for profit and efficiency into the so-called studio system. In the heart of the Depression the coming of sound brought new problems as well as new opportunities to draw in larger and larger audiences. And, to raise local spirits even further, Los Angeles was to be the home of the 1932 Summer Olympics, igniting yet another round of local boosterism and building, even though, in the full grip of the worldwide economic downturn, Los Angeles had been the only city with enough local financial support to bid for the games, and less than half of the eligible international athletes showed up.

The coming of the games to Los Angeles had taken a somewhat hesitant route. In 1921 Los Angeles had campaigned to host the 1924 Olympics but was beaten by Paris, in part because European athletes did not want to travel the long distance. Undaunted, the city tried for 1928, but again lost out to Europe, this time Amsterdam. But the International Olympic Committee was impressed by the Los Angeles representative, as well as by the newly built Memorial Stadium, which had opened in 1923. Finally, in the spring of 1923, the year of the raising of the Hollywoodland sign, the International Olympic Committee announced that the 1932 games would be held in Los Angeles, in part as a nod to the growing athletic prowess of the United States.

Eight years later, when the Olympics finally arrived, the sign itself was also again in the news, for the first time not for reasons of real estate development. On Sunday night, September 18, 1932, the body of twenty-four-year-old Lillian Millicent Entwistle, called Peg, was found in a ravine in the Hollywood Hills below the Hollywoodland sign. According to the *Los Angeles Times* story two days later, in an article headed "Suicide Laid to Film Jinx," Entwistle, who lived with her uncle in a 1913 house several blocks below the stone entrance gates to Hollywoodland, used a workman's ladder to climb to the top of the "H" and jumped off, crashing to the ground and rolling some hundred feet down the steep hillside. A suicide note found in her abandoned handbag read: "I'm afraid I'm a coward. I am sorry for everything. If I had done this a long time ago it would have saved a lot of pain. P. E."

Often when this story is retold, Peg Entwistle is called a starlet, the catchall word for any young woman striving unsuccessfully for Hollywood fame, or, as the screenwriter and novelist Ben Hecht once sardonically defined the word, "any woman under thirty not actively employed in a brothel." But Entwistle hardly seems to have been one of what the director Raoul Walsh called the "profusion of penniless pulchritude" that roamed Hollywood in the late 1920s and early 1930s. In fact she had been a successful star at the Theatre Guild in New York before coming to Los Angeles to stay with her uncle and try her luck in the movies. Nevertheless, the *New York Times* essentially echoed the *Los Angeles Times* story of failed movie aspiration, and both stories included a fetching picture.

In both accounts the story of Peg Entwistle's suicide over despair for not achieving Hollywood success is a foregone conclusion, and some accounts add the grim (undocumented) irony that the day after her death a call to the studio for filming showed up in her mailbox. Yet there are reasons to doubt the traditional tale. Both the situation and her note remain ambiguous. In May of 1932 she, along with Humphrey Bogart and others, was supporting Billie Burke in a new stage comedy. In late July of 1932, she was reported to have been given a contract by RKO on the strength of her performance in *Thirteen Women*, a strange film in which Myrna Loy plays a Eurasian who plots with a swami to kill the girls and their families who treated her badly in school. According to the *Hollywood Reporter* story, Entwistle was "grabbed" after studio executives saw the film. Unless her contract was somehow withdrawn by September, there seems to be no reason why "Hollywood success" was out of her reach, although a contradictory *Hollywood Reporter* story published after her death says that the option "was not exercised [by the studio] when that film was completed." What's going on here? Was she given a contract on the basis of the film, or was it withdrawn on the basis of the film? Entwistle hadn't become a big star, but she wasn't a big star on Broadway or with the Theatre Guild either, just a solid supporting player. If the impulse to suicide was because of recent Hollywood failure, why does her suicide note refer to "a long time ago" when she should have done the deed, and why is she "sorry for everything"? In the account that ascribes her death to failed movie aspiration, wasn't it the fault of studio executives blind to talent? Could there be other reasons for her suicide? In the *Los Angeles Times* article her uncle Harold, himself a minor character actor who often played uncredited roles, pooh-poohs the idea that "a broken love affair had actuated his niece to take her life," although he does briefly allude to her 1929 divorce from actor Robert Keith on grounds of cruelty.

And was it indeed a suicide? Her uncle's house is still there on Beachwood Drive, and if you stand in front of it and look up toward the Hollywood sign, it is clearly a long distance away, three or four miles, up several steep hills, with a final deep ravine to go down and then up even more steeply to the sign, or a circuitous dirt road around the back of Mount Lee. Again according to the

Publicity photo of Peg Entwistle (Courtesy of hollywoodpictures.com)

published story, Entwistle told her uncle that she was going to a drugstore at the little commercial center near the gates of Hollywoodland, and then visit some friends. That trip would have brought her a half mile or so closer to the sign. But the gleaming letters were still far away, up steeply winding streets with no sidewalks, chaparral-covered rocky hillsides, where feet scramble for traction like climbing a sand dune, another fifteen or sixteen hundred feet in the air—not counting the extra feet needed to clamber to the top of the "H," with the help of the conveniently forgotten maintenance ladder. Weren't there other, closer, high places from which she could jump, like the Hollywood Tower apartment building near the foot of Beachwood Drive at Franklin? Did no one who lived on the meandering streets that lead to the sign notice the comparatively well-dressed woman (no sports clothes and running shoes in those days) trudging her way on foot in an area designed only for cars? And where, while all this was going on, was Albert Kothe, the caretaker who kept a supply shack behind the first "L" and made sure that any one of the four thousand bulbs was replaced when it burned out—a task obviously made much easier at night? Could Peg Entwistle have been killed elsewhere and the scene at the sign staged? Was this another crime cover-up so common in the corrupt Los Angeles of the 1930s? Or was she just that resolute to jump, willing to spend the hours it would take climbing the steep hills, and only the sign would do for her springboard to eternity?[1]

All in all, then, regardless of the newspaper efforts to weave a melodramatic story of her "blank despair" over the show business jinx that "dogged her footsteps across the country," there are many unanswered questions about the death of Peg Entwistle. But, as John Ford counsels through James Warner Bellah's screenplay for *The Man Who Shot Liberty Valance*, "When the legend becomes fact, print the legend." So, in the absence of some crucial facts, the legend of Peg Entwistle's jump off the "H" of the Hollywoodland sign remains a dim historical memory, to be revived in the 1970s, like the dilapidated sign itself. In some crucial sense, she is also the presiding genius of this book. Whatever her motivations, she may have been the first to perceive the sign symbolically and make it into a dramatically explicit part of her biography. Appropriately enough, considering the sign's later history, it seemed to take an outsider to notice the sign as something more than just one among many grandiose advertisements that had begun to blanket Los Angeles in those years.

Yet at the time, despite Entwistle's suicide, the sign for most of America and for Hollywood itself remained what it had been at the start—another billboard with no special claim to be the prime symbol of the movie business. The Hollywood brand may have been well established by the 1930s, but not the sign's connection to it. For forty years after Peg Entwistle's death, there is nothing about her suicide in the *Los Angeles Times*, nothing about the significance of her leap from the reproachful sign that first lures and then denies its worshipers, nothing about the haughtiness of people building houses in the Hollywood Hills so that they might be looked up to and look down on others.

The strains of "California, Here I Come," which accompanied the great southern California migration of the 1920s (despite its unfortunate reference to the "golden gate"), still played in the background. But the more relevant song of the 1930s was the mocking "Hooray for Hollywood." The early effort to depict a movie world with open arms for talent didn't last long. As far back as the teens and '20s, the influx of thousands to Hollywood seeking movie fame had been discouraged by the Hollywood Chamber of Commerce in leaflets and advertisements in major newspapers. "Don't Try to Break into the Movies," it cautioned in boldface under a photo of surging crowds outside a movie employment office, "Until you have Obtained *Full, Frank and Dependable Information*," and concluded "Out of 100,000 Persons Who Started at the Bottom of the Screen's Ladder of Fame ONLY FIVE REACHED THE TOP." Even with such warnings, the tide continued. Children were not immune to the infection. The immense success of Jackie Coogan, Baby Peggy, and others in the silent period had started the trend, and when Shirley Temple eclipsed Mae West as the top female box-office star in 1934, the flood of toddlers, tykes, and stage parents just kept coming. Ironically, "Hooray for Hollywood," which debuts in *Hollywood Hotel* (1937), directed by the dance master Busby Berkeley, is less a paean to the wonders of Hollywood than a parody of the people trying to get into the movies. In Johnny Mercer's witty lyrics, Hollywood is the place where mediocrity can be hyped into stardom, "where you're terrific, if you're even good," where even though "you may be homely in your neighborhood," a trip to the makeup man Max Factor can "make a monkey look good." Under its comic flippancy, "Hooray for Hollywood" also aims to shatter the myths of instant stardom that were part of the publicity of the teens and '20s, when some production companies would even advertise for performers, and films made comic fun of the effort to leave small-town life behind for the glitter of Hollywood. This jaundiced view of the lure of the movies continues in several of the Hollywood-set films of the 1930s as well. What had happened?

One crucial change was the coming of sound, which not only undermined the world of the pantomimists, forcing them to adhere to a standard of sounding good as well as looking good, but also undermined the movies themselves, the images on the screen, as an international language and replaced them with the films of a new Babel of national languages. Films that had easily crossed national and linguistic frontiers with just a few easy changes in the intertitles now had to be either dubbed, subtitled, or completely redone—like *Dracula* (1931), whose English-language version was shot during the day, while the Spanish version used the same sets, but a different director and actors, at night. To Hollywood, sound also brought a new surge of writers and actors from theater and the East Coast, as producers struggled to find stars who could talk and writers who could create dialogue and conversation. No longer were the movies the more casual world of the silents, where even stars were expected to supply their own clothes, sometimes with studio stipends, as well as create their own makeup. Few lived in houses, and virtually no one had a car. One of the great chroniclers of California, Carey McWilliams, in his 1946 book *Southern California Country: An Island on the Land,* called Hollywood, because of its history and its separateness from the power structure of Los Angeles, an island within an island. No matter how much it had tried from the start to present itself as the goal of all American dreams, by the 1930s, because of the sensitivity of the sound cameras, sets were now totally closed to casual visitors, and the Hollywood world became even more of an island than ever.

Even though Peg Entwistle in her pain may have had some prophetic sense of what the Hollywood sign would become, its iconic status was still in the future, and it is hardly present in many movies that might otherwise be thought eager to include it. A *Chicago Daily Tribune* story in August 1935, consolingly headlined "Hollywood People Pretty Much Same as Elsewhere," goes back and forth between Hollywood successes (Janet Gaynor's ascent from extra to star) and failures (the recent suicide of Julia Ann Graham, "a dark-haired former choir singer from West Virginia"; two young extras found dead near a statue of Rudolph Valentino) to conclude that Hollywood is a complicated place. The article features a well-populated map of Hollywood and its various outposts, from Tijuana to Malibu, Venice to Palm Springs, without including the Hollywoodland sign. Peg Entwistle is mentioned as part of the article's collection of Hollywood misery, although here the reason for her death is given as "disappointed in a love affair," and her suicide described as leaping "from a huge electric sign overlooking Hollywood." Perhaps the legend hadn't yet reached Chicago, and so the sign went unnamed.

In nearly every one of the Hollywood-focused films of the early 1930s, the most obvious and repeated icon of Hollywood is not the sign but Grauman's Chinese Theatre, with its forecourt of cement-anchored reputations, its premieres with crowds surging to see their favorite stars, and its searchlights puncturing the night sky with their beams. Whatever the reason, Sid Grauman's canny sense of publicity had a role in escalating the national focus on Hollywood as the place of a particular American brand of the intensified personality. Already by 1933, the whole spectacular scene was familiar enough to be gently parodied in Walt Disney's *Mickey's Gala Premiere*, which included caricatures of the Marx Brothers, Laurel and Hardy, Jimmy Durante, and Sid Grauman, winding up with Greta Garbo giving Mickey a big kiss. Hollywood was the beacon, even for a regular guy like Mickey Mouse, who was bashful, but still on stage.

Along with the lavish publicity of Grauman's premieres, the intense public reaction to the death of Valentino in 1926 seems to mark a new phase of the star system, in which certain screen personalities have decisively entered the dream life of their audiences. *What Price Hollywood?* (1932), for example, observes the paraphernalia of the celebrity scene much more closely than similar films of movie-star aspiration in the 1920s. It begins with the old story of a young woman aspiring to be an actress, as an attractive waitress (Constance Bennett) at the Brown Derby puts on her makeup and gets dressed while constantly referring to the picture of actresses in movie magazines. Finally satisfied with her "look," she finishes by pressing her cheek next to a magazine picture of Clark Gable. So the movies both reflect and enhance their own status as the prime etiquette of visible self-presentation in America: what to wear, how to make up, how to stand and act and behave. In the movies was where you wanted to be. Another Hollywood-set film, *Bombshell*, the next year, exposed more of the seamy side of Hollywood ambition, with Jean Harlow as the star and Lee Tracy as her fast-talking, wisecracking publicist, complete with yet another rapid-fire montage of movie magazines. But even with the warning signs, the lure of the spotlight was not going to change.

No doubt a certain amount of this Hollywood self-advertisement, even with its tinge of self-mockery, was aimed to keeping the movie profile up front amid the Depression and the bankruptcies that threatened all and hit some of the studios. *Mickey's Gala Premiere*, among other things, is a blatant promotion for the array of stars it gently caricatures. Like the many vaudeville-type musicals that began the sound period, showcasing what each studio had to offer in the way of talent, the "Hollywood" films of the 1930s often threw together a long list of performers and musical numbers connected with a shred of plot. Part of the lure of these star-stuffed extravaganzas, as it was in the silent comedies of Arbuckle, Normand, and Chaplin, was to see the person behind the role starting to bleed through into something resembling reality—a star who is a strange species of pal.

By the mid-1930s, with the Depression lifting somewhat, at least for portions of the movie business, the tone of self-celebration was even sunnier and included not just Hollywood and its sound stages but also the whole area. A number of shorts about southern California, clearly meant to advertise its charms, were released in 1936, including the travelogues *Los Angeles: Wonder City of the West*; *La Fiesta de Santa Barbara*, with glimpses of Buster Keaton, Ida Lupino, Gary Cooper, and Harpo Marx; and *Private Party on Catalina Isle*, in which we're invited to join Cary Grant, Errol Flynn, and Marion Davies as they get casual and comfortable. But in neither these nor in the somewhat darker looks at Hollywood as the land of artifice and false hopes does the Hollywoodland sign play more than the part of a passing extra. It is frequently absent entirely. *Hollywood Revue of 1929* features chorus girls standing on a sign with the name of the picture in blocky letters that resemble those of the sign, but that's it. Under the credits of *Hollywood Boulevard* (1936) is a rapidly edited array of Hollywood places in which the sign has to share a brief glimpse with the Brown Derby, the Chinese Theatre, the Griffith Observatory, the Broadway department store, as well as the street and its pedestrians and traffic—the montage creating a seemingly cohesive image of a Hollywood world that doesn't really exist, by juxtaposing places miles apart.

A little later two Warner Bros. films have glimpses of the sign, first as part of an implausible set depicting "Gower Gulch" in *Thank Your Lucky Stars* (1943); and then, in reality, as part of a pan across Hollywood in *Hollywood Canteen* (1944) at a point in the story when wounded soldiers from the South Pacific arrive in Los Angeles in search of the famous club of the title. In *Hollywood Canteen* also, I should note, the pan ends with a shot of the soldiers at the corner of Hollywood and Vine. As far as the rest of the country was concerned, that intersection was a more emblematic place for the period than the by-now tattered sign itself, although the reputation of Hollywood and Vine came primarily from the invisible world of radio, because so many shows originated nearby. It was also considered by many to be the most disappointing sight in Hollywood, since the fantasy was so far from the mundane reality.

On the soundtrack during that first look at Hollywood in *Hollywood Canteen* is Richard Whiting's rousing music for "Hooray for Hollywood," but without the lyrics, a prophecy of how the song will be treated once it becomes an anthem rather than a parody. Its original source, *Hollywood Hotel*, named after the hostelry first built by H. J. Whitley to accommodate potential real estate investors and later the early movie business migrants, con-

The sign as seen in *Hollywood Boulevard*, 1936

tains no image of the sign. Nor does the most memorable of all the Hollywood-set movies of the 1930s, *A Star Is Born* (1937). If by number of appearances in films and postcards we judge the most iconic of Hollywood landmarks, the palm has to go to the Hollywood Bowl, neck and neck with the Chinese Theatre.

Hollywood Boulevard and *A Star Is Born* also share a characteristic Hollywood-oriented theme of the 1930s: the has-been actor. In the decade or so from the more innocent teens and '20s to the more skeptical 1930s, the Hollywood plot has shifted from the aspiring migrant, giddily seeking movie fame, to the has-been, keeping up pretenses while scraping the bottom for any role he can get. Both of these films play between these intertwined themes of Hollywood success and failure. Intriguingly, as in such otherwise carefree early musicals as *Forty-second Street* (1932) and somewhat more serious films like *What Price Hollywood?* (1932), the pattern is the fall of an outmoded male figure, sometimes a director, sometimes an actor, and the rise of a new female one, almost always an actress.[2]

Hollywood Boulevard's treatment of the story is more satiric and light-hearted as befits its travelogue-like view of southern California, which includes not only Hollywood and Los Angeles but also Santa Barbara as a major setting. It begins with a montage of all the stars who have imprinted their feet and hands in the cement of the Chinese forecourt (a tradition that Grauman started with Fairbanks and Pickford in 1927). A little girl asks her mother what the emcee means by calling this making "an immortal mark in Hollywood." The mother answers that it means that the new star having the cement treatment "will be known forever." In the crowd, however, is John Blakeford, a great star in his day but now unrecognized by anyone, who gets his picture in the paper only when he's sued by his tailor for unpaid bills. Owing everyone around town, Blakeford reluctantly accepts an offer from *Modern Truth*, a movie scandal magazine, for his memoirs. Blakeford wants this to be high-minded, but is persuaded by the publisher to include stories of his love life, which are then embroidered and invented by writers at the magazine, to feed the "insatiable desire" of the American public "to read about the private lives of public personalities." This doesn't sit very well with his ex-wife and daughter, who have moved to Santa Barbara to get away from the Hollywood life. Robert Cummings as a Hollywood-addled scriptwriter who falls for the daughter and learns the error of his showbiz ways completes the major characters in the plot.

The satiric touch of *Hollywood Boulevard* is undeniable, but its lush locations in Malibu and Santa Barbara, along with its frequent references, visual and verbal, to Hollywood nightspots like the Brown Derby, the Trocadero, and Ciro's, shows a total affection as well. And the theme of the has-been Blakeford, who finally redeems himself in his daughter's eyes, gets an odd turn by the inclusion in the film of several actual silent stars still clinging to the edge of Hollywood celebrity and recognizability, including Francis X. Bushman, Maurice Costello, Esther Ralston, and Mae Marsh—most of them totally unfamiliar to movie audiences today. Hollywood history in a sense has moved into its second generation and, with few exceptions, those who made their mark in silents have been erased by sound.

A Star Is Born, which takes much of its basic plot from *What Price Hollywood?* made five years earlier, has a darker tone, telling the story of an aspiring actress fruitlessly making the rounds to agents and Central Casting, then being discovered by an old Hollywood star who marries her and watches as her career explodes and his fizzles. Even without the fan magazine subplot of *Hollywood Boulevard*, it nevertheless teases the audience into trying to guess which real stories it is fictionalizing, by beginning with the

script page for the film and an "any resemblances are coinciden-
tal" disclaimer, which both foregrounds the artifice of filmmaking
and tempts the viewer to try to see behind the scenes. That the star
is Janet Gaynor, who began as an extra and later won the first
Oscar for best actress in 1929, only tantalizes further.

Like the silent film plot of the midwestern girl who longs to
be a star, Esther Blodgett (Gaynor) from North Dakota has a
fantasy of "Hollywood," fed by her worship of the actor Norman
Maine (Fredric March). Her father and aunt disapprove, but her
grandmother, seeing a parallel between Esther's desire "to be
somebody" and her own pioneer past going west, gives her the
money to go and find "your Hollywood." When Esther gets to
Hollywood, after feeding her dream by stepping into Norman
Maine's footprints at the Chinese, she discovers that her fantasy
is hardly unique. There are masses of people with the same desire for stardom. Like the main character in *What Price Hollywood?* she meets the well-established Maine when she is a waitress at a party, after seeing him drunkenly abusing a photographer
at the Hollywood Bowl. He fosters her career, and then, as her
star rises, like so many of the other men in these films he becomes an embittered alcoholic, finally committing suicide. Even
though at the end she will, at least for the moment, give up her
movie name of "Vicki Lester" and identify herself as Mrs. Norman Maine, no one could mistake the underlying idea that
Hollywood and stardom are still presented as the source of her
"real" identity. But its dual view—it's great to be a star but you

have to be a person as well—kept resonating with audiences as the basic armature of all show business biography from at least *Pagliacci* onward: success onstage, heartache offstage. *A Star Is Born* was the top moneymaker of the year, winning two Academy Awards (for original story and a special award for color photography), with several other nominations as well. It was remade twice, including Judy Garland's 1954 comeback film, for which she insisted on having George Cukor as her director, who had also directed *What Price Hollywood?*

If we consider the Hollywood-set films of the 1930s, especially after the middle of the decade, the darkening side of the Hollywood experience seems more prominent or at least more interesting than the bland celebration of the many star-studded but inane films by which studios tried to prove and keep proving that they had the actors and actresses the public wanted to see. This more skeptical view was perfectly encapsulated by Nathanael West in *The Day of the Locust*, published in 1939.

> The edges of the trees burned with a pale violet light and their centers gradually turned from deep purple to black. The same violet piping, like a Neon tube, outlined the tops of the ugly, hump-backed hills and they were almost beautiful.
>
> But not even the soft wash of dusk could help the houses. Only dynamite would be of any use against the Mexican ranch houses, Samoan huts, Mediterranean villas, Egyptian and Japanese temples, Swiss chalets, Tudor cottages, and every possible combination of these styles that lined the slopes of the canyon.

The murky shadows that the legend of Peg Entwistle's jump from the sign cast over the Hollywood story of the 1930s were also mirrored in the jaundiced attitude toward Hollywood of the many journalists, novelists, short-story writers, and playwrights— a few of them native and many more transplants from the East Coast—lured there by easy screenwriting money. The first wave of the migration had started in the 1920s, when foreign directors like Ernst Lubitsch, Victor Seastrom, and Michael Curtiz, and stars like Greta Garbo, Nita Naldi, and Pola Negri were brought to Hollywood to confirm its international power. The second wave came in the 1930s and early 1940s, as artists of all kinds fled Hitler's sway, many coming to Hollywood and by their presence bringing an international flavor to the American film industry: Billy Wilder, William Wyler, Fritz Lang, Jean Renoir, and many others.

On the whole, the European newcomers paradoxically looked at Hollywood and Los Angeles with a less cynical eye than the East Coast migrants did. Perhaps because they saw less differ-ence between Hollywood boosterism and ballyhoo and their own goals for the film business than did the products of the gritty writer's life of Chicago, Detroit, and New York. Not that Los Angeles was in any way immune from grit and corruption, although when films showed mob activity they tended to set the story in Chicago or New York, even while gangsters were gain-ing power in Los Angeles in the person of figures like Mickey Cohen and Bugsy Siegel.

But for many of the writers the issue wasn't crime or no crime, rain or sunshine, it was that elusive idea called authenticity. As West in *The Day of the Locust* implies with his attack against the conglomeration of housing styles, Los Angeles was fake, not real like the history of the East. West, it must be said, did have a touch of compassion for the benighted Angelenos. The passage above continues:

> It is hard to laugh at the need for beauty and romance, no matter how tasteless, even horrible, the results of that need are. But it is easy to sigh. Few things are sadder than the truly monstrous.

Well, I did say a touch.

West, born in New York, was one of a group of East Coast writers who came out to Hollywood with the advent of sound to try their luck in the film business. Sound meant dialogue rather than brief intertitles, and the studios were reaching out to any and all sources of writing talent, primarily from journalism, prose fiction, and theater. West lived in a variety of places in Hollywood, first as a night manager in a small apartment house north of Hollywood Boulevard, only a few blocks from Beachwood Drive. As *The Day of the Locust* shows, he was fascinated by the lower depths of the Hollywood scene, and frequently hung out with other writers at the former bootlegger Stanley Rose's art gallery and bookstore on Hollywood Boulevard, next to the Musso & Frank Grill. Not far behind the restaurant in West's day still stood L. Frank Baum's Ozcot. Although there's no evidence West knew this, there's an interestingly jagged line to be drawn between the more sunny utopias of the Oz books and the darkly shadowed dystopia of West's view of Los Angeles. It culminates in *The Day of the Locust* with his hero Tod Hackett's vision of his grandiose painting "The Burning of Los Angeles," and the book's final event, a riot at a premiere at "Kahn's Persian Palace Theatre," a scene that has been said to have been inspired by the 1930 premiere of *Hell's Angels* at the Chinese.

West published his novel in 1939, at the end of the decade, but his hostility to the eclectic architectural style of the homes of southern California had been presaged early on by writers such as Edgar Rice Burroughs. In *The Girl from Hollywood* (1923), which appeared in the midst of the scandals of the early 1920s, Burroughs seemed to associate the general corruption of the movie colony with its corrupt architectural taste: "The bungalow at 421 Vista del Paso was of the new school of Hollywood architecture, which appears to be a hysterical effort to combine Queen Anne, Italian, Swiss chalet, Moorish, Mission, and Martian." The same attitude was reflected and elaborated beyond invective by another set of artistic migrants who arrived in Los Angeles in the 1920s: the modernist architects led by Rudolf Schindler, Richard Neutra, and others. Leaving Europe to work early on for Frank Lloyd Wright, whose aesthetic was hardly devoid of ornamentation, Schindler and Neutra pushed their ideas for domestic architecture more toward Le Corbusier's idea of the "machine for living," but mixed with a California openness and flow between inside and outside that Corbusier never managed. Out with stucco and sculpted window frames, and any stylistic detail that evoked earlier architecture. The past was over. This anti-historical side of architectural modernism appealed as well to many of the self-made Hollywood immigrants who often commissioned these houses—"I am uncaused and original"—not springing from the earth but laid upon it. The future had clean lines and paid the past no mind. In addition to dreams of the past, Los Angeles was becoming the focus of avant-garde dreams as well. One type of originality might go back to roots and origins, while another claimed to be unprecedented.

What was the authenticity by which the modernists judged these past efforts of the imagination—an imagination not unlike their own—but an aspiration they could feel no bond with? West sensed that it was an architecture of yearning, yearning for a connection to a past, to something grander and more romantic than the present. But his more usual attitude, like that of many of the East Coast transplants, was disdain. The architects had even less mixed feelings. Writing in 1946, when the revulsion against the architectural eclecticism of the 1920s and after was still at high tide, Carey McWilliams praised the modernists for "rebelling against all gimcrack ornament, cheap construction, and false effect." Frank Lloyd Wright was brought in to hammer the point home: "Thought or feeling for integrity had not entered into this architecture. All was flatulent or fraudulent with a cheap opulent taste for tawdry Spanish Medievalism." Richard Neutra even more explicitly indicts the movies as the aesthetic villain: "Motion pictures have undoubtedly confused architectural tastes. They may be blamed for many phenomena on the landscape such as: Half-timber English peasant cottages, French Provincial and 'mission bell' type adobes, Arabian minarets, Georgian mansions on 50 x 120 foot lots with 'Mexican Ranchos' adjoining them on sites of the same size." Neutra was so visually upset by the architectural mélange of Los Angeles that, according to one story, he and his wife bought a Nash Rambler, the first American car to feature seats that reclined, specifically so that, while she drove, he could lie prone and not have to see the revolting march of architectural hybrids whizzing by.[3]

The tension between ostentation and hiddenness, the allusion to past styles as a mode of creating both social and aesthetic status, the flow between interior and exterior, the sensuosity of the domestic environment, a house shaped to the bodies that live in it—all these characteristics of earlier Los Angeles architecture were seen by many transplants from the East, as well as by the early European modernists, as the absence of authenticity. Like West, Neutra in his own way aimed toward a kind of impossible purity by which this pastiche world of domestic fantasy must be harshly judged. But even though their disdain was similar, the motivation of the modernists was different. West seems to want an authenticity that he associates with the more "real" past of the East Coast and especially New England, while Neutra aims toward a future unburdened by anything that came before.

■

Even though Hollywood the place, the subdivision of Los Angeles, boasted plenty of premieres, theaters, and an increasingly tattered Hollywoodland sign in the 1930s, it was still not an important center of movie making. As early as 1915, mindful perhaps of the general distaste many Hollywood citizens felt for "the movies," Harry Culver offered free land in his new development for anyone who would establish a studio there. Thomas Ince, Samuel Goldwyn, Hal Roach, and others quickly took him up on his offer. In 1937, the heads of the Chamber of Commerce along with other Culver City activists circulated petitions in an effort to rename the area "Hollywood" because so many more movies were being made there. In response the Hollywood Chamber of Commerce threatened to secede from Los Angeles to become a separate city once again and safeguard its name, keeping the teapot boiling. The Culver City group replied that it would take the name "Hollywood City" to differentiate itself from any other nearby Hollywood. Finally, the *Los Angeles Times* reported, the conflict between the two was settled by literally burying the hatchet in one of those concrete slabs "in ceremonies in the forecourt of Grauman's Chinese Theater."

More practically, the Los Angeles City Council shortly thereafter passed Ordinance 78,499, which gave Hollywood new and expanded boundaries, extending to Doheny Drive on the west, the Los Angeles River on the east, and Melrose Avenue on the south, neatly including a host of studios that were otherwise on the periphery of Hollywood or beyond its old official limits. One chronicler of Hollywood history has written that this was done "for reasons never adequately explained" and was "shrugged off by many as a typical bureaucratic aberration." But the need to maintain the core Hollywood brand and its historical location in the face of potential controversy and dilution was clearly uppermost in the City Council's mind. Los Angeles needed Hollywood and Hollywood needed Los Angeles. Thanks to these expanded boundaries, if not that many movies had been made in the confines of old Hollywood, they would be now.

In these same years that the status and meaning of Hollywood as the center of the movies was being threatened by those who claimed a greater justification for their own towns to be called "Hollywood," the physical situation of the sign changed as well. Buffeted by storms until it lost its "H"—the same letter that Peg Entwistle supposedly jumped from—the sign read "OLLYWOOD-LAND" for several years. Mack Sennett went into bankruptcy in 1933 and the mansion one of his biographers calls his "Xanadu" was never built. But the leveling of the top of the notorious summit in the Hollywood Hills once called one of the Three Sisters was suitable for other purposes. As the second highest peak in the Hollywood Hills and the highest accessible by road, it was a perfect place for transmitting the new world of radio and later television into the San Fernando Valley and beyond.

Don Lee, a pioneering California broadcaster, previously the owner of KFRC in San Francisco, had a Cadillac distributorship in downtown Los Angeles, where he also built a radio station, taking over KHJ from the *Los Angeles Times*, and in 1931 began transmitting the experimental television station W6XAO, the only one west of the Mississippi. Lee died in 1934, the year after Mack Sennett went bankrupt with the collapse of Paramount-Publix, in which he was an investor. As he writes in *King of Comedy*, "I lost the studio, the mountain, the acres of land in Los Angeles." Interest in television was growing at the time, and Lee's son, Thomas S. Lee, bought some twenty acres of Sennett's Rancho Providencia property for a new telecasting station, including studios and a swimming pool for employees. The mayor inaugurated the new site, which had been renamed Mount Lee in honor of the pioneering communication work of the elder Lee, who had not coincidentally been a longtime friend of Sennett. Like the Eiffel Tower, which was saved from destruction as a temporary structure by its use for communication during World War I, the threadbare Hollywoodland sign got its own reprieve when Mount Lee became a similarly crucial center in World War II. Still later, in the early 1950s, it became part of the cold war Civil Defense network as a regional control center.

Perhaps because the land above was now devoted to the Lee

studio and transmission tower, or perhaps because Hollywood-land needed the money more than the publicity, regular maintenance on the sign was stopped entirely in 1939. It was a world different from when the sign was erected in 1923. Thanks to Prohibition and the closeness to the Mexican border, organized crime had become more established in southern California, gambling boats plied the seas just off the Santa Monica coast, and studio unions were often infested with and run by gangsters. Scandal magazines, like the fictional *Modern Truth* in *Hollywood Boulevard*, titillated their readers with behind-the-scenes stories of movie-star sin, and gossip columnists like the great forerunner Louella Parsons and her later rival Hedda Hopper became king- and queen-makers, catered to by stars and publicists alike. Hopper, in the words of the Hollywood historian Gregory Paul Williams, was "as conservative and prudish as a Wilcox-era resident."[4] She began her career in 1930, the same year that saw the appearance of *Modern Screen*, and called her Beverly Hills home "The House that Fear Built." By the end of the 1930s there was no uncompromised or uncritical "Hooray for Hollywood." No wonder the lyrics were dropped. Champions and critics alike argued over whether Hollywood was the quintessence of America or the prime seat of the subversion of American values. Censors of all sorts as well as reformers saw the power of the movies and tried to co-opt it for their own purposes, while high on a hill above them all the Hollywoodland sign sat tottering on its telephone pole legs, sheet metal letters hanging awry, silent.

FOUR

Shadows on the Sign

This was Hollywood, California, in 1915, with its sun-kissed
oranges and lemon groves, before it was visited by the Three
Horsemen of the Apocalypse—oil, movies, and aeronautics—who
strode the earth, uprooting the orange and the lemon trees,
and in their stead built factories and movie picture studios.
I was one of the offenders.
—CHARLIE CHAPLIN, *How to Make Movies*

Chaplin's chronology in this introduction to the 1930s version of
his account of the building of his first studio is a little off. Oil was
discovered in Los Angeles in 1902, and perhaps he could have
added cattle and real estate to the other transformers of the
southern California landscape. But his sense of the changes in
Hollywood and Los Angeles was right on target. Despite our
contemporary nostalgia for 1939 as the year of great movies,
along with the official dubbing of the Academy Award as the
"Oscar," the 1930s were not ending well for Los Angeles, Hollywood, or the sign that proclaimed "Hollywoodland." It may have
been the high-water mark of the studio system, but there were
more than enough jaundiced eyes, politically and aesthetically, to
counter that optimism. The government enforcement of the

so-called Paramount Decree, which led to the breakup of studio control over distribution and exhibition as well as production, was on the near horizon (although not fully implemented until after the war). And a small group of talented writers were raising the previously somewhat trashy genre of the Hollywood novel to new levels of literary intensity: 1939 saw the publication of Nathanael West's *The Day of the Locust*, Raymond Chandler's *The Big Sleep*, John Fante's *Ask the Dust*, and, if we expand the category to novels that feature California as the Promised Land, John Steinbeck's *The Grapes of Wrath*, winner of the Pulitzer Prize. In 1940 came John Ford's film version of *The Grapes of Wrath*, and the next year Budd Schulberg's *What Makes Sammy Run?* and F. Scott Fitzgerald's posthumous *The Last Tycoon*. In the minds of Dust Bowl refugees, California may have seemed the same fruitful mecca it had always been in the American imagination. But as Woody Guthrie's song had it, "California is a garden of Eden, a paradise to live in or to see, / But believe it or not, you won't find it so hot, / if you ain't got that do-re-mi." And these darker visions of the movie business and of Los Angeles itself told another side of the story.

By the 1940s southern California was no longer, as it had been in the nineteenth and early twentieth centuries, the prime refuge of those looking for health and delaying death. Early Hollywood had tried to keep out various evil-smelling and noisy businesses by ordinance, pushing them to the south and east. Los Angeles had tried to do the same. But war contracts and new industry supporting the war brought more prosperity and jobs to southern California, along with new inhabitants: African-Americans from the South and Midwest looking for war industry jobs; military men and women who had shipped out of Los Angeles to the Pacific and decided to return there to make their homes; engineers and technicians from all over lured by the aircraft industry. The war had encouraged a new migration, this time of much younger people to the West Coast—people who came looking for opportunity rather than retirement, and people who sought to escape the prejudices of their small towns. These prejudices weren't only racial and religious, but also sexual, as gay and lesbian members of the armed services found a more open atmosphere, and Los Angeles in the postwar period became the setting for early gay rights organizations like the Mattachine Society and One, Inc. The Los Angeles created between the wars was changing for good. Between 1940 and 1950 there was a 31 percent increase in the population of Los Angeles City, a 49 percent increase in Los Angeles County, and a 65.4 percent increase in Orange County, where so much industry was located.

But with the industry and the opportunity came the smog. As Chaplin foresaw, the lemon and orange orchards of Hollywood had for the most part vanished, except for the few trees adorning backyards and for sale in nurseries. The old orange-crate emblems of sun-kissed southern California were considered archaic and stuffed away in the backrooms of garages and junk shops. They could not even be revived as collectibles until the next wave of nostalgia hit in the 1970s, as did the taste for Spanish

Colonial Revival and all the other housing styles mocked by Nathanael West and the modernists. By the 1940s, in place of the clear-aired, golden world of the past image of Los Angeles came dark skies, rain, trench coats, and a miasma that closed up the throat and bleared the eyes. Instead of the sunny Southland of the earlier part of the century, so beloved of boosters, this was the gloomier vision of both Hollywood and Los Angeles foretold in *The Day of the Locust* and *Ask the Dust*. As Raymond Chandler put it in *The Lady in the Lake*, "The weather was hot and sticky and the acid sting of the smog had crept as far west as Beverly Hills. From the top of Mulholland Drive you could see it leveled out all over the city like a ground mist. . . . Everybody was griping about it. . . . Everything was the fault of the smog." The crucial date when even the most rabid booster could ignore the smog no longer was September 8, 1943, or, as the local newspapers called it, "Black Wednesday."

According to the Oxford English Dictionary, the word *smog* was first used in 1905 to refer to the special murky atmosphere of London, although the coal-dust-filled London fog had been described long before in the novels of Charles Dickens and Robert Louis Stevenson's *Dr. Jekyll and Mr. Hyde*. But by the early 1940s "smog" was being regularly and almost exclusively applied to the choking atmosphere of Los Angeles, and it had become one of the most usual clichés in descriptions of the city. However, even though the word might not have been used, if we recall how the Hollywoodland ads promised a relief from the smoke and fog of the city, the concept was there long before, to signify the crowded, evil-smelling urban world from which prospective buyers in the Hollywood Hills needed to escape. A new prosperity had energized Los Angeles, but along with it came stinging eyes, headaches, and ash-strewn patio furniture.

The war brought other changes in the atmosphere of Hollywood and Los Angeles more benevolent than smog. *Hollywood Canteen*, the 1944 film that includes a quick pan across the Hollywoodland sign to settle on a shot of soldiers back from the Pacific on Hollywood Boulevard, celebrated the institution founded by Bette Davis, John Garfield, and others in the fall of 1942 to serve the thousands of military personnel going in and out of Los Angeles on their way to and from the Pacific war. Like coastal ports elsewhere, Los Angeles was losing something of its own parochialism as it played host to draftees and officers from all over the country, who in their turn discovered something of life in the big city.

Comedians like Mabel Normand, Fatty Arbuckle, and Charlie Chaplin had always seemed closer to the real life of their audiences than distant silent idols like Theda Bara and Rudolph Valentino. The stars of the 1930s, whose glamour was chronicled by the fan magazines and gossip columnists, were even more distant luminaries, created and coddled by the studio system in full flight. But the war brought them down to earth, as a kind of democratic aristocracy, in whose ranks the normal citizens of the

United States (and the world) could read enlarged versions of themselves. For the most part, they joined the various branches of the service just like the average Joe, even though a few got fancier commissions, and some studio executives strutted around in custom-made uniforms. But in the war films ordinary heroism was being celebrated, not star glitter, and so it was in the Hollywood Canteen. *Hollywood Canteen* the film helped its bottom line as well, since the canteen received 40 percent of its profits, with an advance of $250,000, the equivalent of almost $3 million today. A parallel institution was the Hollywood Guild and Canteen, the outgrowth of a philanthropic group organized in the late 1930s to help "the less fortunate persons connected with the picture industry," but which then found a new, more all-embracing cause with the war. Presided over by Anne "Mom" Lehr, by the closing year of the war she had rooms and meals for up to twelve hundred servicemen a night.

In addition to those beds and three squares at the Guild and Canteen, that ordinary Joe could also hobnob at the Hollywood Canteen with an incredible array of actors, actresses, and film personnel, all volunteering their time to support the troops. In one emblematic scene in *Hollywood Canteen* a soldier is being taken by a hostess to the food table: "Say, aren't you Jane Wyman the actress?" he asks. "Well, let's just say I'm Jane Wyman, period," she replies. Still confused about the atmosphere of egalitarian mingling, he continues, "You work here too?" "Evenings," she deadpans. "Migosh, I thought movie actresses got paid enough not to work at night." Somewhat later an even more hapless soldier is dancing with a young woman and trying out his pickup line: "You know, you're a dead ringer for Joan Crawford." "Am I really?" she says diffidently, but then after a few more steps decides to be open. "Don't look now," she says, "but I *am* Joan Crawford"—whereupon he faints.

Hollywood may have taken off its high hat and changed its wartime image to a more democratic "we're all in this together" look. But the Hollywoodland sign's status as a possible symbol of this new community remained fleeting. With the end of regular maintenance in 1939 and the wartime focus on Mount Lee as the home of militarily crucial communication towers, the tangible presence of the sign became a source of continual controversy for those local politicians and activists who cared. In 1945 the 455-acre site was donated to the city by the M. H. Sherman company, and in 1947, after the Los Angeles Recreation and Parks Commission had wanted it razed to the ground as an irrelevant eyesore, the Hollywood Chamber of Commerce protested and offered to refurbish the sign, restoring the "H" and removing the "LAND."

Change was in the air. Harry Chandler had died in 1944, but C. E. Toberman had finally paid off his Depression development debts in 1946, and was ready to take advantage of the postwar boom. The Hollywood Freeway, built between 1947 and 1949, was one of the first urban renewal projects to be completed after the war, originating in downtown Los Angeles, slicing through old neighborhoods, and taking the motorist over the Cahuenga Pass and into the San Fernando Valley. If you were traveling north from Los Angeles on this particular piece of Highway 101, you had an extended view of the old Hollywoodland sign. What better time to dust it off and set it up to greet the new postwar world?

Supporting the Chamber of Commerce's proposal was city council member Lloyd C. Davies, whose district included the sign. A longtime promoter of Hollywood, Davies was interested in cleaning up Hollywood in other ways. The same year, he was instrumental in getting an ordinance passed against the "degenerates" who he said were infesting the neighborhood. To top off his drive for Hollywood purity, he did the narration for a Republic film titled *The Red Menace*, in which he played a small part as an immigration inspector.

After a brief legal tug of war, the city attorney approved the Hollywood Chamber of Commerce's proposal to drop the "LAND" and make the repairs to the rest of the sign, so long as all construction was done entirely at the Chamber of Commerce's expense and the city was indemnified for any liability. All told, the Chamber of Commerce ultimately spent some five thousand dollars, and at least for the moment the sign was saved from destruction. Almost unnoticed, an important milestone in its history had been passed. For the first time, it read "HOLLYWOOD," not "HOLLYWOODLAND." From then on that is how the sign is referred to in newspapers. So, in one sense, in January of 1949, the Hollywood sign was born, or perhaps reborn. Like a phoenix, it would have a few more rebirths before it became the icon we now see.

At the same time that the sign was getting a fresh coat of paint and some necessary repairs, council member Davies's effort to clear the way for the renovation of the sign, along with his cold-war paranoia about "degenerates" and Communist infiltration, marks an intriguing transformation in the image of both Hollywood and Los Angeles. After the wartime explosion of moviegoing and the commitment of Hollywood to the war effort, the postwar period saw a closing down on all fronts, as Hollywood began an era of running scared. The peak attendance year in history was 1946, when Americans went to the movies in a percentage of the population that would never be exceeded. Then, in 1947 the House Un-American Activities Committee (HUAC) made its first visit to Hollywood to pursue the investigation of Communist influence in the movies, leading to the infamous blacklist. In the same year the first regularly scheduled television programs were beginning to appear. In such an embattled atmosphere the need to assert "Hollywood" was obvious, and the Chamber of Commerce's move to take charge of the sign was in direct response to the political threat from Washington and the cultural threat from that entertainment interloper, television.

In films as well the studios were fighting back, with Cinerama, 3-D, Cinemascope, VistaVision, and a host of other technological wonders aimed to show that the living-room box came in dead last when it was a question of color and spectacle. In 1949, as "LAND" was disappearing from Mount Lee, MGM added "Made in Hollywood, U.S.A." to its closing logo, in part perhaps because it was celebrating its twenty-fifth anniversary but also because of the need to reassert the Hollywood brand in the face of potential audience defections. The fact that MGM's production facilities had been and were still in Culver City was cheerfully ignored, although some of the activists who wanted to change that city's name to "Hollywood" twelve years before may have noted the irony.

MGM also was a central player in the resurgent effort to celebrate Hollywood as the culmination and apotheosis of all the entertainment of the past, the inheritor of all previous art forms. If the theme song of the 1920s was the exuberant "California, Here I Come" and of the 1930s the gently mocking "Hooray for Hollywood," the theme of the 1940s and 1950s was that paean to the indomitable spirit of the entertainer, Irving Berlin's "There's No Business Like Show Business." It had been sung three times in *Annie Get Your Gun*, the play of 1946, and given its most spectacular setting in the finale to the film version of 1950, when all of Buffalo Bill's Wild West Show joins in. At the same time, *Annie*'s story of the ignorant backwoods sharpshooter who becomes a star reprises with a sentimental glow the seductions of the show business world and its special brand of community. Song- and dance-filled biopics of songwriters, composers, musicians, singers, and impresarios of the past flooded out of the studios in what often resembled a replay of that urge to respectability that pre-occupied movie executives in the teens and '20s. "We are part of a great American artistic tradition," seemed to be the message, as warm-hearted views of the nineteenth-century Broadway past (*Easter Parade, The Belle of New York*) rubbed shoulders with revivals of 1920s operettas (*The Desert Song, The Merry Widow*). To top off the nostalgic celebration came that satiric but loving evocation of the early film business, the still preeminent salute to Hollywood's own history, *Singin' in the Rain*.

But lavish Technicolor tributes to the great stars and events of show business history weren't the only subjects for films in postwar Hollywood, however much they typified prestige productions by studios like MGM and Warner Bros. Emerging from the shadows like a guilty conscience came a darker sense of the present. While some of the studios were fighting off the threats of Washington and television with lavish spectaculars celebrating the glorious past, other studios (or the same ones in a different mood) were delving into social problems like alcoholism, teenage delinquency, racial and religious prejudice, and organized crime. In these films, from the mid-1940s on, the image of both Hollywood and Los Angeles was often indistinguishable from that of other big cities, principally New York and Chicago. As the Okies had found out, instead of open arms, California could be a place of rejection and hostility. Down these mean streets Chandler's detective Philip Marlowe walked, or drove, as Chandler meticulously detailed the streets of the labyrinth, the paths through the city, from the tenements of the poor and down and out to the mansions of the rich. They were all part of the complex web of Los Angeles life that the detective needed to know in order to discover the sinister truth of the crime. The promise of utopian visions and fairyland castles had turned into substance-less trash. As Chandler remarked as early as 1939 in *The Big Sleep*, "About the only part of a California house you can't put your foot through is the front door."

John Fante's view in *Ask the Dust* doesn't partake of West's brand of urban apocalypse, but it is similarly pessimistic. Setting his story of an aspiring writer like himself in the early 1930s, he nevertheless also foresees the spreading blight: "I went to my room, up the dusty stairs of Bunker Hill, past the soot-covered frame buildings along the dark street, sand and oil and grease choking the futile palm trees standing like dying prisoners, chained to a little plot of ground with black pavement hiding their feet." Instead of the Los Angeles of Hollywood stars, fancy houses, and custom-made cars, Fante's downtown Los Angeles, like West's collection of Hollywood Boulevard grotesques, is a world of the downtrodden and dispossessed, the ones who came to search for health, happiness, and success, but found instead only a new emptiness: "Smith and Jones and Parker, druggist, banker, baker, dust of Chicago and Cincinnati and Cleveland on their shoes, doomed to die in the sun, a few dollars in the bank, enough to subscribe to the *Los Angeles Times*, enough to keep alive the illusion that this was paradise, that their little papier-mâché homes were castles." In the next literary generation, Fante's exploration of lowlife Los Angeles would greatly influence Charles Bukowski.

By the mid- to late 1940s this sense of disillusionment with the dream seeped into the movies in the form of a style and mode of storytelling called film noir. In an odd way the noir films represented a triumph of Hollywood. Just as World War I had opened the way for Hollywood to become a major world power in film production because of the virtual shutdown of the European film industry, World War II repeated the economic and cultural favor. Hollywood films flooded the European market so thoroughly that after the war various European countries instituted protectionist laws that required the American importation of a certain number of their own films for every Hollywood product brought across the pond. Unlike the aftermath of World War I, which saw a migration of European filmmaking talent to Hollywood, the new situation after World War II not only strengthened the European film industries but also gave rise to whole new generations of filmmakers whose work created a kind of international film culture unparalleled since the silent period.

As the European and Japanese film industries revived, Hollywood itself had to take notice. The Cannes Film Festival began in 1946, offering an elaborate alternative to the Academy Awards. The next year the first Foreign Film Oscar was awarded to Italy for Vittoria De Sica's *Shoe Shine*, and later winners in the following decade included Akira Kurosawa, René Clement, Federico Fellini, and Kon Ichigawa.

Intriguingly, a great part of the inspiration for many of the new non-"Hollywood" filmmakers were the Hollywood films they had seen during the war and after, not so much the gaudy spectacles as the dark and gritty little B pictures. To describe them, French film critics Nino Frank and Jean-Pierre Chartier in 1945 invoked a term used to describe France's own dark films of the late 1930s—film noir. In noir films the city was less a paradise than a confusing maze, a rainswept Los Angeles of dark alleys and frustrated dreams. The studio system may have been booming, Humphrey Bogart may have had a salary large enough to compete with presidents and CEOs, but in noir the image of the actual place where the dream factory turned out its wares was as tattered, decrepit, and insubstantial as the Hollywood sign that stood so shakily above it on the hills. Like the detective story, noir was a city genre and a city perspective on the world, paranoid, fatalistic, gloomy, and even on occasion apocalyptic. Its tone was indebted less to the sunshine vision of Los Angeles than to the urban troubles that convulsed the city during the war: the mass expulsion of Japanese-Americans to internment camps in 1942; the Sleepy Lagoon case of the same year, in which six hundred Mexican-American young men were arrested in connection with a murder and nine convicted, only to have their convictions reversed two years later by the California Supreme

Court; the Zoot Suit riots of 1943, in which young male members of minority groups were attacked by white servicemen who considered them slackers. The wartime image of Los Angeles was not the swank and glitter of Hollywood so much as ethnic conflict spiced with the occasional mysterious and gruesome murder, like that of Elizabeth Short, the Black Dahlia, murdered in 1947, drained of blood, cut in half, left on a hillside in southern Los Angeles, and given a nickname based on the 1946 Alan Ladd movie, *The Blue Dahlia.*

Many of the films influenced by this gloomier atmosphere of ethnic conflict, urban social change, and violent crime begin with an airplane or helicopter-eye view of the city at night, complete with glittering neon and brightly lit skyscrapers, then swiftly descend to the streets and alleys for their stories. Sometimes the city was New York, often Los Angeles, with less frequency Chicago, although the visual signals of their urbanness were similar. But rather than the 1930s-style celebration of Hollywood Boulevard and its clubs and theaters, noir usually presented a grittier image—the flophouses of Bunker Hill, the rickety funicular of Angel's Flight, the dreary industrial landscape of factories and gas storage tanks.

Consider, for example, the 1944 film *Murder My Sweet*, based on Chandler's 1941 novel *Farewell My Lovely*, which retains something of the flavor of its Los Angeles setting, especially the closeness to nature. In the beginning Philip Marlowe sits in his office at night, musing on the gaudiness of the neon city. Later he will go on a shady errand into the hills, be startled by a deer, and then knocked unconscious. Finally, he faces the murderer in a beach house on a cliff. Although the paths through the city are intricate, there is always a sense that the city itself has been constructed as an artificial barrier against the natural world that comes bubbling up in the form of passion and murder. From the God's-eye view of the beginnings of many of these films, with their enticing patterns of darkness and light, we descend to a seeming small city, even a neighborhood, filled with fatal coincidences, happenstance meetings that thwart human aspiration and will. It may rain rarely in Los Angeles, but it rains often in film noir. In terms of the Hollywood sign, the noir films set in Los Angeles, with their unblinking focus on the griminess of the cityscape, might be considered almost explicit rejections or repressions of the safety and comfort the original real-estate sign promised. No one looks up to the sky or the peaks where the sign might be found. This is an underground world, or a barely aboveground world, where hopes and dreams are invariably shattered or thwarted, usually beyond repair. When the rare film, like *Down Three Dark Streets* (1953), does wind up at the Hollywood sign, it's for a shootout that indicates how the corruption of the city below has managed to cover the hills as well.

The 1950 film *He Walked by Night* stays more resolutely in the city than does *Murder My Sweet*. Under the credits and at the end of the film is a large map labeled "City of Los Angeles Metropolitan Area." Then we see a view of Los Angeles from the

The sign in the climax of *Down Three Dark Streets*, 1953

Hollywood Hills, looking not toward them (where the sign might appear) but away, down the rectilinear grid of streetlights and buildings. Although this Los Angeles has clearly become a megalopolis, there is little grandeur in the image. When we come to the story, which begins in an electronics theft, we find not an epic crime and a imposing criminal, but a small man outside the law, who kills an off-duty policeman who suspects something. The rest of the film is taken up with the chase for the elusive criminal, as the police department deploys all its scientific resources and manpower to find him. In much of the film he is literally underground, racing through a network of sub-basements and sewers whose connections he knows and the police have to trace. Again, as in many of these films, Los Angeles street names and addresses play an important part, as do recognizable parts of the city, buildings, and intersections. The underground stream of the Rio Hondo, the nature that the city has buried, runs through some of these sewers, and the detectives poring over the maps frequently cite the names of streets that anchor the events in a particular geographic place. The pseudo-documentary style of many of these films, their concentration on police procedures and laboratory work, imply that this is the way Los Angeles really is, not the glitter and spotlights, but the concrete sidewalks and trash-filled gutters. As Jack Webb, who had played a police lab worker in *He Walked by Night*, lugubriously intones at the beginning of *Dragnet*, the 1949 television police series created virtually in tandem with the Los Angeles Police Department: "This is the city."

Not that Los Angeles or Hollywood had given up the booster megaphone entirely in the 1950s. A February 1953 story in the *Los Angeles Times* trumpets "Southland Lure Brings Notables; Record Seen." Los Angeles is still a magnet, readers are reassured, for the rich seeking warmth. As the subhead elaborates, "Leaders in Every Walk of Life in Los Angeles for Winter; Hotels Crowded," and a good chunk of the article is devoted to the listing of their notable and prosperous names. A general migration to southern California was also unabated. At the middle and lower reaches of the social ladder, postwar home building was filling in many undeveloped areas to the south of Los Angeles, helping to create that nightly neon grid pattern that introduces so many noir films. It could be called the second neo-rural period of Los Angeles. Now it was the orchards and vegetable fields to the south that were being dug up and turned into tract housing, sometimes designed by high-minded young architects, and promoted by social reformers as part of a new democracy of small affordable one-family homes to welcome back the millions of veterans and offer a solution to the housing shortage.

But these latter-day efforts to create a new vision of social utopia in southern California ran aground on the rocky shoals of cold-war paranoia. The Case Study houses commissioned and promoted by *Art and Architecture* magazine, based in Los Angeles, were built in areas like Mar Vista, far to the west of Los Angeles. Developers and opponents of public housing on the Los Angeles City Council attacked the City Housing Authority by publicizing the "communist affiliations" of its information director, Frank Wilkinson, and claiming that he was the spearhead of Communist infiltration into public housing. In the context of similar accusations about Hollywood and the Los Angeles school system, these charges effectively doomed public housing in Los Angeles for years to come, while Fletcher Bowron, the mayor who defended the housing authority, was defeated at the next election, thanks in part to the daily hostility of the *Los Angeles Times* to his "leftist" inclinations. The area that had been designated as the site for the housing, Chavez Ravine, later became the home of Dodger Stadium.

In contrast to the innovative architecture of the Case Study houses, the most popular style of private housing was overlaid with a heavy coating of nostalgia. This was the ranch house, a southern California housing style born and bred with a bit more original authenticity—that difficult concept!—than the Spanish Colonial and Mission Revival styles of the past. Originally designed for the new West Coast suburbs, it turned out to be as suitable for the commuters of the East Coast who could take the train home from "the city," be picked up by the wife in the family station wagon with its faux wood paneling, relax with a drink in the knotty pine rec room, and turn on the television to watch *Gunsmoke* or *Frontier Playhouse*. After the war, the creation of suburbia in the image of the Old West reflected a pervasive national mood. Leaving the city behind, the pioneer family, fed on old Hollywood movies and television westerns, had kids named Beaver, and duded up Junior's bedroom with Hopalong Cassidy lamps, toy chests, and quilts. Without attics and, in California, often without basements, the ranch house aimed at a future unburdened by a real past but half in love with an imagined one.

One intriguing difference between the cozy ranch house and the palatial homes of Hollywoodland stands out. Whereas the houses of Hollywoodland, like the sign itself, faced outward toward the light, emphasizing their own prestige along with the flow between inside and outside, the ranch house tended to turn inward, toward the conversation pit and the backyard barbecue, the family refuge. Here then was another phase in the metamorphosis of the Hollywood and the Los Angeles ideal—another definition of leisure and wholesome family life, now carried by western movies, with their longing for the open and freer world of the past, and by the television sitcom families that lived out a comic version of the dream in sunny fictional suburbia.[1]

Was this return to the thrilling days of yesteryear a retort to the dark present of film noir, or was their simultaneous popularity just another of the usual paradoxes of cultural change? The 1940s and '50s might be called the Dorian Gray period of Hollywood. The studio system seemed to be thriving, even in the face of television, but it was being constantly patched and repatched behind the scenes. The lavish Technicolor versions of old Broadway and old Hollywood took place on studio sets and for the most part embraced their artifice as a luscious escape. Other depictions of the Hollywood present were less celebratory. Schulberg's *What Makes Sammy Run?* and Fitzgerald's *The Last Tycoon* in the early 1940s had given a literary imprimatur to the novel of behind-the-scenes Hollywood scandal and failure. No longer was it only the stars who were the source of scandal. Now it was the previously insulated producers and owners of studios. Norman Mailer's *The Deer Park* (1955), dealing with the time he spent in Hollywood after the success of *The Naked and the Dead* (1948), was another significant moment in this new tradition of ripping away the veil of movieland respectability. At the same time *Confidential* magazine took the usually tepid revelations of the gossip columnists to a new level, or depth, with its monthly exposures of extramarital hanky-panky and exotic sexual tastes.

Films also began to feature behind-the-scenes Hollywood settings, often with a predatory and corrupt mogul as a central figure. Could this more savage portrait of the buccaneers of the Hollywood past now be painted because so many of the founding moguls had either died or been eased out of their jobs? By the 1950s, studios had become more obviously businesses rather than personal fiefdoms. The period of the great Hollywood magnates was drawing to a close, and with it some of the allure of the old pioneering movie world. Its unique combination of brutality and vision was also disappearing. Like the noir films and unlike the upbeat musical biopics, films like *The Bad and the Beautiful* (1952) took a cynical view of the Hollywood system. There had always been a sneaking admiration for the entrepreneurial energy of the pirates of the past, but it now seemed to have soured completely. The founders are dead in *The Bad and the Beautiful*, and their inheritors can't live up to them. The roman à clef of the plot lets us see in Lana Turner's star drunkard father a caricature of John Barrymore, while the evil mogul father of Kirk Douglas resembles Harry Cohn. Young Douglas is ruthless enough himself, but all in the service of vindicating his father, and he works in the mode of the poorly appreciated but creative producer Val Lewton, with cheap sets and shadows.

The has-been actor, which was a new Hollywood character type in the films of the 1930s, also makes a comeback, in perhaps its greatest version: Gloria Swanson's Norma Desmond in Billy Wilder's *Sunset Boulevard* (1950), her name a complex tribute to Mabel Normand, Norma Talmadge, and the ill-fated William Desmond Taylor. But the postwar version of the burdens of the Hollywood past treats the still-living remnants of that past with much less kindness than did *Hollywood Boulevard* some fifteen years earlier. Like the detective novelists and the documentarians, Wilder sets his story in a recognizable Los Angeles, complete with well-known buildings and street addresses. Here, as in his earlier film *Double Indemnity* (1944), Wilder insists on an acute sense of place to anchor his story of people who basically live in the past, immortalizing Los Angeles as the neo-realists were immortalizing Rome; and as the New Wave, a few years later, immortalized postwar Paris. In this contemporary Hollywood world, complete with scenes in Schwab's Drugstore and the Alto Nido apartment house, the Hollywood past in the person of Norma Desmond and her friends is viewed as both outmoded and demented. Gloria Swanson may have been all of fifty-one when the film was released, but as far as the story goes we are a couple of cinematic generations down the years from the time of Norma Desmond's flourishing. Betty, one of the characters, had a grandmother who did stunt work for silent serial star Pearl White. Her father was a studio electrician, and her mother still works in wardrobe.

The elaborate Mission-influenced look of the interior and exterior of Desmond's mansion, the baroque hangings, the invocations of innumerable past worlds of style—everything that was so up-to-date in the 1920s—is now only a source of ridicule. No longer a vital world, this is the decayed Hollywood of the past, in which Desmond lives like Miss Havisham in Dickens's *Great Expectations*, waiting for the young suitor, the prospective husband who never showed up at the altar, in this version an out-of-work screenwriter who will take his place. Meanwhile Swanson/ Desmond is surrounded by some of the great figures of the past: Erich von Stroheim plays her butler, while Buster Keaton, Anna Q. Nilsson, and H. B. Warner appear as her card-playing cronies, stiffly sitting around her table like waxworks. The whole atmosphere resembles a gothic horror movie, with living corpses who have outlived the screen immortality Hollywood promised. Only Cecil B. DeMille survives from that distant past; he at least is still working. But for the most part it is the ghoulish atmosphere that defines the memory of Hollywood past, and few if any mourn the decaying grandes dames and leading men of yesteryear. Like Norma Desmond herself, coming down the stairs at the end of the film to tell DeMille she is ready for her closeup, they were considered self-absorbed, over the top, and possibly crazed remnants of a past best forgotten.

In fact, it was a time when mansions like Desmond's were either subdivided, their elaborate coffered and stenciled ceilings painted over in white, or torn down, like the mansion in *Sunset*

Boulevard itself. Owned by the first wife of J. Paul Getty, it made its last movie appearance in *Rebel Without a Cause* (1956), which especially featured its darkly archaic interior, along with its empty and moss-scarred swimming pool. Another kiss of death to the old style of Los Angeles domestic architecture was administered by Alfred Hitchcock's *Psycho* (1960). Instead of the house of horror being a gothic castle or a decrepit English country estate, it was that apple of the early Hollywood settler's eye, the elaborately tricked-out Queen Anne–Eastlake home, with its painted shingles, its dome, and its seemingly inviting porch, now darkened with the colors of terror, suitable only to be a haunted house.

In some symbiotic way, the decaying sign above the city mirrored the attitude toward Hollywood's own history. In *Psycho*, of course, the past lays a heavy hand on the present, but it is a past filled with murder and madness. Otherwise, what use was the past, whether it was the past in architecture or the past in Hollywood history? Who cared what pleasure Chaplin, say, had given to his public now that some considered his political views too left-wing and liberal, and J. Edgar Hoover pressured the Immigration and Naturalization Department to revoke his reentry privileges while he was in England for a short trip? Who had the better deal—Chaplin in exile from Hollywood in Switzerland, or Keaton, frozen-faced at Norma Desmond's table? Both, it seemed, in their different ways belonged to a past best forgotten.

Would the Hollywood sign suffer the same fate? Unlike the

Dorian Gray portrait of the studio system, the sign couldn't be kept deteriorating in the closet, while its shiny exterior faced the world. Instead it was falling apart in plain sight, despite the periodic care of paint and tin Band-Aids courtesy of the Hollywood Chamber of Commerce and a few hardy donors. But notwithstanding a general lack of interest from the official film world, the Chamber of Commerce soldiered on. Another Hollywood initiative of the 1950s designed to burnish the town's and the industry's image was the Hollywood Walk of Fame. First broached in 1953 by E. M. Stuart, then head of the Chamber of Commerce, the Walk of Fame became a major project of the Chamber's Hollywood Improvement Association spin-off and was finally officially dedicated in time for Hollywood Boulevard's Santa Claus Lane Parade in the fall of 1960, as part of a "multimillion dollar program to make Hollywood Southern California's top tourist drawing card"—a brave boast, especially since Disneyland was already in operation since 1955.

Stretching out from its beginnings at Hollywood and Vine, still considered the center of Hollywood despite its radio-spawned invisibility, the Walk of Fame featured four-foot terrazzo squares in the trendy pink and charcoal gray colors of the period (more usually seen in dress shirts and knit ties), in which the celebratory stars would be placed. As the *Los Angeles Times* proclaimed, "Hollywood's appearance will soon be as glamorous as its name." And of course there was also the obligatory grandiosity of the project: "the biggest terrazzo pour job ever undertaken."

Six names of stars chosen by lot started off the project, which grew over time into thousands. Some notable names, however, were left out. Charlie Chaplin had been nominated for an early star, but was turned down because of his "moral turpitude and communist sympathies." In 1960 his son Charles Chaplin, Jr., sued the Hollywood Improvement Association, but the case was thrown out of court. By the early 1970s, however, tempers had cooled and cold-war attitudes had waned enough that the Chamber of Commerce voted Chaplin a star despite the negative recommendation of its own executive committee. The chamber had perhaps been encouraged by the fact that Chaplin was to receive a special Academy Award that year for his contributions to the growth of the motion pictures. Nevertheless, nasty letters poured in to the chamber, the Motion Picture Academy, and the *Los Angeles Times*, but all still went as planned, and Chaplin received a five-minute ovation at the Oscar ceremonies. In 1978 another Walk of Fame controversy erupted when Los Angeles mayor Tom Bradley, a former policeman and the first African-American mayor of the city, protested the Chamber of Commerce's refusal to give Paul Robeson a star because of his political sympathies. This time action was much quicker, and Robeson, who had died three years before, received his star less than a year later.

FIVE

From Eyesore to Icon

"Who saw the Hollywood sign first?"
"Me!"
"When?"
"When I was five."
"I saw it when I was a baby."
"How do you know?"
"My parents took me up to 'servatory and
they said I pointed to it."
—Overheard at the Fern Dell playground in Griffith Park

There are icons by accident and icons on purpose. Mount Rushmore and the Statue of Liberty were built to be iconic, the focus of attention and meaning. But Big Ben or the Eiffel Tower, like the Hollywood sign, accrued meaning over the years. Before World War II, for example, the significance of Big Ben was more local. But with the war its proud tower rising over the smoke and bombs of the Battle of Britain became a symbol of British fortitude generally and of London specifically. As we've seen, wars and the aftermath of wars particularly are a fertile field for newly grown icons to flourish. Uncle Sam existed as an image since the nineteenth century. But it was James Montgomery Flagg's World War I poster depicting the character's top hat, pointing finger, and stern expression—"I Want You for U.S. Army"—that made him a nationally recognized and widely imitated icon. Similarly, in the visual imagery of the mobilization effort for World War II, the Liberty Bell, the Statue of Liberty, and Uncle Sam played even wider roles than before. Icons like these create a sense of symbolic coherence and common purpose, whether it's for a people girding to fight a common enemy, or for an industry or a city in danger of fragmenting.

The Hollywood Chamber of Commerce and the Hollywood Improvement Association had struggled mightily to maintain and improve the image of a neighborhood that was suffering the same blight that had come to older urban areas across America. But as far as the Hollywood sign was concerned, it was an uphill battle. The physical Hollywood existed as a place with legally determined boundaries. But the name Hollywood had become an abstraction, a metonym that seemed to refer to everything about the movies except for the town that supposedly gave them birth. Hollywood as a brand had become international, but Hollywood as a collection of streets, buildings, and memories still needed a lot of work. Although newspaper stories referred to "the famous Hollywood sign" as a "tourist mecca" with some frequency in the postwar period, the sign was basically a dilapidated wreck. The 1949 removal of "LAND" and the reconstruction of the "H" by the Chamber of Commerce had staved off total collapse for a while, but more renovation was needed. The 1970s would become the decade in which the sign would bloom again, rising from its tattered remnants to become the icon we see today.

The beginnings of its resurrection were homegrown but not very auspicious. The Hollywood Kiwanis Club paid for yet another refurbishing at the start of the decade, but by a few years later further deterioration had set in, despite the naming of the sign as Los Angeles Historical-Cultural Monument #111 in 1973. Even so, its new status was a bit of an afterthought in Hollywood landmarks: ten years after the Hollywoodland Gates had been named, five years after Grauman's Chinese Theatre, and four years after the Charlie Chaplin Studios on La Brea. Early in his term, State Senator David Roberti, who represented the area from 1971 to 1994, proposed that the sign be named a California Historical Landmark, but that elevation went nowhere.

By 1973, however, the effort to remake the sign found a new momentum. A few years before, MGM auctioned off all the props and furnishings from its Golden Age, seeming to signal the final collapse of the old studio system. But then the "New Hollywood" of Steven Spielberg, George Lucas, Francis Coppola, Martin Scorsese, and others began to renovate the idea of a Hollywood movie, and there came into being one of Hollywood's periodic bouts of nostalgia. The sign was its prime beneficiary. Restoring the sign would revive Hollywood as a place, a focus, a vital node in Los Angeles and American culture. In the spirit of the times, one sarcastic writer even complained about the ridiculousness of the urge to preserve the sign while the city and its inhabitants were blithely going about destroying the rest of Hollywood's past, while another mockingly called it "a legend in its own grime." Nevertheless, a "Save the Sign Committee" and a "Friends of the Hollywood Sign Committee" were formed and both proceeded to have benefits and fund-raisers. One prominent celebration included a showing of the new Hanna-Barbera film of *Charlotte's Web*, perhaps appropriately for this effort to reconstruct a word on a hill, since in the story Charlotte saves Wilbur the pig from slaughter by the messages she weaves in her web.

The Hollywood Chamber of Commerce aimed to raise fifteen thousand dollars, and Billy H. Hunt, the executive vice president of the Alliance of Motion Picture and Television Producers, was the most prominent public face of the movement. But despite what might seem to be the leverage of his position, Hunt finally managed to scrape together only some fifteen hundred dollars from seventy-three film companies, a pittance compared to the ten thousand dollars donated by R. Leslie Kelley, the auto dealer who founded the Kelley Blue Book car-rating service. Once again it seemed as if the automobile dealers were more invested in the iconic significance of the sign than the denizens of Hollywood, although Billy Hunt was eloquent about the need for a symbol to pull together what in the 1970s was rapidly becoming a wildly decentralized industry.

Whereas most of the financial supporters and cheerleaders for the renewal of the sign were local and even neighborhood in origin, the story about the sign's need for repairs went around the world—an early indication of its potential significance as the iconic representation of the movies in general. The *Glasgow Evening Citizen*, the *Johannesburg Star*, and the *Djakarta Indonesia News* all carried articles, along with the same picture of the threadbare sign, complete with the crumbling top of one "O" and a "D" so tattered that it threatened to become a backward "C."

Contracts were let for repairs to an optimistic builder who estimated the work would take a little over two weeks, although he hadn't planned on the workers who quit the first day because the site was too steep and the weather too hot. Anyone who has skittered precariously down the hill to the sign and then laboriously climbed back up through the silty yellow earth, small rocks, and patches of chaparral could sympathize. The job in fact took five weeks, and sign-gazers from below were titillated by what was called the sign's "disappearance" when green primer covered the letters and blended them invisibly into the hillside. In September of 1973 the job was done, in time for a gala premiere, complete with floodlights. Gloria Swanson, who had so bravely played a caricature of the silent-screen diva in *Sunset Boulevard*, did the honors of the unveiling. All went well, despite some loud local residents, upset with the constant run of heavy traffic up their narrow winding streets, who brandished placards saying "Death to the Sign" and "Down with the Sign."[1]

That would seem to be that: Sign restored, admiring political dignitaries, movie star presence, and an explicit link to the glories of Hollywood past. But all the patching and strengthening and sealing and repainting weren't enough to defend the sign against wind and weather, let alone the numerous locals who were still using the area as a picturesque iconic backdrop for their late-night parties of dope and booze. By only a few years later the repairs were beginning to show their age. In 1976 KIIS, a local radio station, sponsored a Save the Sign campaign and raised four thousand dollars for yet another in the series of quick fixes that had been going on for almost thirty years. By 1977 it was clear that only a major overhaul could work. Early in the new year the Hollywood Chamber of Commerce invited a group of media "personalities" up to the sign to launch yet another effort. Participants were issued Official Boy Scout snakebite kits just in case they met some of the reptiles whose ancestors Mack Sennett's mother's pigs had failed to flush out. But even with the support of a prominent disc jockey and Joel Wachs, a City Council member, the director of the Hollywood Chamber of Commerce was hardly sanguine about the prospects for the sign's future: "What we really need now is a guardian angel."

More than a year later, still looking for that guardian angel, the Honorary Hollywood Sign Committee had a gala event at the Hollywood Roosevelt Hotel to kick off the sign-rescue yet again, with an invitation featuring an image of the sign with its now crumbling third "O." Council member Wachs was honorary chairman of the committee and Lucille Ball was its official spokesperson. Public officials and Hollywood figures like Ernest Borgnine, George Stevens, Jack Valenti, and John Wayne lent their names as well. Finally, it seemed, there was enough political power and star power to get the job done.

∎

Why did the 1970s mark the time when, after years of neglect, there was enough appreciation of the idea and potential significance of the Hollywood sign, enough widespread support, and especially enough money made available to reconstruct the sign and turn it into the icon it has become today? One crucial factor was a newly awakened sense of the history of Los Angeles and of Hollywood that was revealed in a variety of ways, not the least of which was the keen although often distorted sense of Hollywood history portrayed in films like *Chinatown* (1974). Instead of the decayed Los Angeles of 1940s and 1950s film noir, this was a nostalgic version of the 1920s and 1930s. As modernist architecture itself aged, the past that modernism had rejected had become more intriguing, and its ornaments, instead of being condemned as inauthentic, became a sign of individual taste and authenticity combating the faceless machine civilization of the future.

More tangibly, some groups in Los Angeles had embarked on an effort to recognize and understand its past, publicizing the need to develop ways of preserving that past from demolition and redevelopment. In 1962 a Cultural Heritage Board had been created that quickly set to work blocking plans to demolish landmarks and drawing up lists of buildings that should be preserved for the future. Even earlier there had been a significant argument over a Los Angeles landmark that helped raise the local consciousness of the need to preserve historical structures that may have been behind the political decision to create the board in the first place. The structure in question was not an adobe from the Californio period or a Queen Anne–Eastlake home from the 1890s or a monument of Neutra and Schindler modernism. It was Simon Rodia's monumental personal creation, Watts Towers.

Watts Towers first appeared on the horizon of Los Angeles civic awareness in the early 1950s, when it was nearing its completion. Starting in the 1920s, Rodia, a tile setter who lived by the Pacific Electric tracks in south-central Los Angeles, had created an enormous architectural pastiche of everyday objects— plates, tiles, bottles, cans—all embedded in a concrete fairyland of swooping curves and soaring pinnacles. An early *Los Angeles Times* article in 1952 struck a patriotic note appropriate for the period in its headline: "Immigrant Builds Towers to Show His Love for U.S.," detailing Rodia's effort to include references to Columbus and Joan of Arc, along with designs recalling Indian and Spanish motifs. In 1959, however, the Los Angeles Building and Safety Department was not impressed by either Rodia's art or his patriotism. Declaring the towers a hazard—Rodia after all had no formal engineering background—the department proposed to tear them down as a danger to the public.

What happened instead was a spur to action reminiscent of

the Hollywood Chamber of Commerce's response to the city's desire in 1947 to tear down the Hollywood sign. At first the *Los Angeles Times* was somewhat snide about the people who rallied to thwart the city's will, noting that "A cross section of artists, architects, students, engineers, with a seasoning of beatniks, thronged the hearing room." But soon the controversy expanded. Parts of the hearing were televised, and from across the country and around the world came a wave of support from admirers of the towers. Los Angeles, the city of the future, was being taught, by both its otherwise ignored insiders and a host of prestigious outsiders, that it had a past worth preserving. Falling back on its narrow expertise, Building and Safety then insisted that the towers be tested. A ten-thousand-pound weight would be used in an attempt to pull the highest tower out of plumb. In October 1959 the towers passed the test with flying colors. As the *Times* art critic wrote, it was a "sign of this city's cultural maturity that the fight for the Watts Towers was made and won." In 1961 a Towers Committee, made up of interested citizens, was formed as a watchdog organization. Four years later the same city that had tried to destroy the towers declared them a Cultural-Historical Monument, a decade before the sign received the same honor.

Whatever lessons about pride in civic history had been learned in the controversy over Watts Towers, however, the Watts riots of August 1965 emphasized that the present-day Los Angeles was hardly in the best shape. Instead of a positive image of enlightened civic awareness of the cultural wealth in its midst, Watts in national news stories was accompanied instead by photographs of clouds of billowing smoke from burning stores and armed soldiers patrolling the streets, inspiring the painter and political activist Irving Petlin to recall Nathanael's West's grim prophecy in *The Day of the Locust* with a four-part painting called *The Burning of Los Angeles, 1965–67.* Finally, in 1975, after a state bond issue backed preservation efforts, the city as custodian of the funds went to work on keeping the towers renovated, under the watchful eye of the Towers Committee. It was the same year that the first new housing since the 1965 riots was built in Watts. Now deeded the towers by the Towers Committee, in 1978 the city in its turn then deeded the towers to the state of California, although they were still operated by the Los Angeles Municipal Arts department on a fifty-year lease. Almost immediately the Center for Law in the Public Interest sued the city for not maintaining the towers properly, and the next year the California Supreme Court ordered the city to return all funds to the state, which would take over the job. Finally, in the early 1980s the state allocated $1 million for repairs and renovation, and the establishment of a Los Angeles Cultural Affairs Department made the continuing life of the towers a priority.

Despite its many complications, the early fight for the preservation of Watts Towers was an amalgam of elements that helped set the stage for the renovation of the Hollywood sign: another transformation of what some considered an eyesore into a recognized icon. Watts Towers was a distinctive structure created not by famous architects but by an untutored Italian immigrant, sited in a lower-class African-American neighborhood, and not made of the finest materials, but pieced together from the detritus of modern life, discarded containers, odd pieces of metal, and whatever else caught Rodia's eye as he walked along the railroad tracks. The Watts Towers therefore combined the populist and crowd-pleasing with the most avant-garde areas of American art, and the Hollywood sign was beginning to assume a similar pedigree.

With the late 1950s and early 1960s the inclination to abstraction that was the most pervasive style of postwar American art was gradually giving way to a more representational form that included abstract elements but also drew on popular and vernacular imagery. One version of this movement that potentially opened the eyes of critics and appreciators of high art to the treasures around them were the assemblages of Robert Rauschenberg, incorporating everyday found objects and images culled from magazines, advertisements, and otherwise "low" forms of visual representation. Rodia's similar amassing of what others had thrown away to create the towers preceded Rauschenberg's by many years, but the changes in artistic perspective that Rauschenberg's work represented made Rodia's masterpiece more "visible," eccentric in origin perhaps, but an eccentricity that had in the intervening years become mainstream.

Even more directly related to the Hollywood sign, however, was the advent of Pop Art—works that drew upon advertising, signage, and comic books to create a partially ironic, partially celebratory view of the normal visual surroundings of modern life inflated like circus balloons as a challenge to high-art pretentiousness. After the polemical attack against the depiction of objects and figures in abstract expressionism, cartoons and superheroes and soup cans had suddenly become acceptable subject matter, their iconic familiarity connecting the new artistic avantgarde to the real life of a mass audience.

Certainly, a combination of words and images had previously been used in art, as had assemblage, especially in the Cubist period by artists like Pablo Picasso and Georges Braque. But it was more in the American mode to use signs and billboards, as did many American realist painters and photographers of the 1930s: Edward Hopper in his painting of two women in a restaurant with a large bulb-studded sign out the window (*Chop Suey*, 1929); or Walker Evans, in photographs where the uplifting billboard is sometimes ironically juxtaposed with the human sadness nearby ("Houses and Billboards, Atlanta, 1936").

But it was in southern California, with its legacy of the intermingling of advertising, artifice, and nature that Pop Art flourished most elaborately. In 1962 the Pasadena Museum played host to a bellwether exhibition, "New Painting of Common Objects," that included such artists as Andy Warhol, Roy Lichtenstein, Jim Dine, Wayne Thiebaud, and Ed Ruscha. Warhol, with his background in advertising, drew directly on brand names in works like his Campbell Soup cans and Brillo boxes. Artists were creating art that at first appeared to be a branch of commerce, but, as in the movies, the line between art and commerce was becoming obscure in the art world itself.

While some artists turned the normal objects of sight into hyperreal forms, others pushed the interest in heightening the everyday more in the direction of abstraction. Ruscha, whose earliest artistic aspiration had been to be a cartoonist, had moved to Los Angeles in 1956 and in 1961 painted *Large Trademark with Eight Spotlights*, which included a stylized Twentieth Century–Fox logo along with the kind of premiere illumination pioneered by Otto Olesen for Sid Grauman. Ruscha has often disingenuously disclaimed a Los Angeles and Hollywood influence on his work, but his use of billboard words and supergraphics, along with his early preoccupation with the Los Angeles landscape in photographic books like *Twenty-six Gas Stations* (1963) and *Every Building on the Sunset Strip* (1966) imply otherwise. In the late 1960s he began a series of paintings and silkscreens of the Hollywood sign, in part, he has said, because he could see it from his studio on North Western Avenue and just decided to paint it: "I would look up there, and I began to use it as a smog indicator. If I could see that sign, I would figure that the smog was not so bad. . . . I began making drawings and paintings of it, and a silkscreen print of the image with sort of fictitious skies of my own design." Meanwhile, during the same years, other artists were similarly exploring the iconic features of the Los Angeles landscape: David Hockney in the stylized realism of paintings like *A Bigger Splash* (1968), Richard Diebenkorn in his abstract

Ocean Park landscapes, and Claes Oldenburg in whimsical draw-ings like "City as Alphabet."[2]

The absorption of brand names into works of avant-garde art emphasized what was intangible about the whole idea of brand-ing and advertising. Beyond its physical reference to a soup can, a piece of steel wool soaked in cleanser, or the name of a neighborhood in Los Angeles, the brand conveyed a glamorous atmosphere more than a specific concrete object. Like the rela-tion between a movie star and the human being who bore the star's name, its repeated images beckoned the viewer—and the customer—to a world beyond itself. The result was not just a hearty meal or a clean frying pan, but what was starting to be called a lifestyle. Like advertising in general, the brand implies that it will supply something that is crucially missing, something still to be attained, an ideal vision of life.

No wonder perhaps that a ragged sign sitting high on a hill-side might seem to be the quintessence of brands, for those who knew where to look. Far from its origins as a way of attracting new homeowners, the Hollywood sign began to stand for the eternal American quest, which in California had first meant gold, then health, and now a vague but alluring personal enrichment that included them all. Does it matter that Ruscha's images of the sign don't really resemble the sign very much at all? His "HOLLY-WOOD" sits on the ridgeline, whereas the actual sign is of course below the ridge, framed by the hillside. In fact, some of Ruscha's images, especially the ones in red, much more resemble the Outpost Canyon sign, with its red neon letters and its ridgeline perch, than they do the Hollywood sign. But the greater importance of Ruscha's work, like the work of the Pop artists and assemblage artists in general, was the way they refreshed the eye. Just as the housing styles dismissed by West and Neutra and so many others as ugly and ersatz gained a different kind of authenticity as they aged, so the sign, previously ignored as the decrepit remnant of a past Hollywood housing boom, another ugly mark on the landscape, another elephantine example of Los Angeles and Hollywood grandiosity, somehow began to be seen not as what it originally referred to but as a piece of art in itself, making it visible in a way it could not have been before.

The advent of television as well as the attacks of the House Un-American Activities Committee helped to create a defensive self-consciousness that led the Hollywood Chamber of Commerce to explore the iconic possibilities of the Hollywood sign. Similarly, the residual local shame the Watts riots of 1965 had brought to the city helped inspire efforts to re-create Los Angeles in terms of its cultural monuments. More and more articles began to appear in Los Angeles area newspapers guiding the reader on tours of prominent architectural and cultural sites. Throughout the 1960s, Los Angeles was waking up to its own history and amassing a hit parade of its prime landmarks to be earmarked for protection and celebration. By the early 1970s the Cultural Heritage Board had put the Hollywood sign on a list of protected places that ran from the adobes of the distant past to the already celebrated gems of California modernism. A local sense of Los Angeles history had finally arrived, which would issue in the founding of the Los Angeles Conservancy in 1978, the same year that the Hollywood sign was recast in much the same form that we see it today.

The critical mass of civic pressure to refurbish the city's image was helped along nationally by films and television focusing on Los Angeles and Hollywood as settings. In television especially, the tradition of folksy camaraderie between ordinary people and stars that started in the Hollywood Canteen took on new forms, especially emphasizing a more sunny suburban side of the area in contrast to the grim stories set in downtown Los Angeles. In *I Love Lucy*, perhaps the most popular television show of the 1950s, the Ricardos move to Hollywood to help Ricky's career, and episodes frequently feature Lucy in escapades involving her efforts either to get on television herself or to persuade a star to participate in one of her schemes. In *Ozzie and Harriet*, which ran from 1950 to 1966, there were also frequent exteriors of the Nelson family house on Camino Palmero, just off Franklin (and across the street from the former estate of C. E. Toberman). Another vehicle for this "just folks" view of the show business community was the late-night talk show, especially the *Tonight Show*, hosted by Johnny Carson, which in 1972 moved from New York to Burbank in the San Fernando Valley.

The movies, still highlighting Hollywood, went in two somewhat different directions. One was the period film, like *China-*

town (1974) or *The Day of the Locust* (1975), based on West's novel, bringing a touch of romance back to old Spanish-style buildings and the neighborhoods.[3] In these, the sign rarely if ever appears; the lure is Los Angeles of the 1930s, as it is in *City of Angels*, the 1976 television detective series, which began with a montage of vintage photographs. There was even in the early 1970s an attempt to revive the Peg Entwistle story as a stage musical by Dory Previn in *Mary C. Brown and the Hollywood Sign*, which went into rehearsals but was never finally produced. Written in the wake of the breakup of Previn's marriage to André Previn, precipitated by Mia Farrow, it now exists only as a song album (1972), shedding an intriguing light on the original story, since a failed love affair was specifically denied by Entwistle's uncle as a cause of her suicide. Appropriately enough, Previn's song is quoted in a *Los Angeles Times* article in 1973—the first time in more than forty years that Peg Entwistle was in the news.

Curiously, the other mode of the Hollywood-set film of the 1970s and after was the disaster film. In earlier apocalyptic films like *The War of the Worlds* (1953), the iconic building subject to direct Martian attack is Los Angeles City Hall, while in the noir classic *Kiss Me Deadly* (1955), the atomic explosion that will presumably destroy most of southern California begins in a Malibu beach house. But in the 1970s, whether the attack is from an outraged nature, a band of aliens, a megalomaniac criminal, or an inept schlemiel, the Hollywood sign features prominently. *Earthquake* (1974) helps begin the trend. *The Day of the Locust*

(1975) neatly combines the apocalyptic film with the period film, as does *1941* (1979), which, like *Rocketeer* (1991), supplies a whimsical reason for the loss of "LAND" from the sign. But perhaps the most emblematic of all is *Blade Runner* (1982), which manages to combine the aura of 1920s Los Angeles with the dystopian vision of a genetically engineered Los Angeles of the near future.[4]

What connection might there be between the gradual resurrection of the Hollywood sign in the 1970s and the appearance of apocalyptic disaster narratives, in which the sign, like other icons, is destroyed or damaged? First is the coming of a movie shorthand by which certain structures are considered to be the emblems of their cities. With the globe-trotting adventures of the arch-spy James Bond in 1962 (*Dr. No*), as well as other less memorable characters and films, the need to quickly establish a foreign or exotic setting becomes a Hollywood necessity. Filming such a place from airplanes could do it, but helicopters were even better. The helicopter was a product perfected in World War II, and mass-produced helicopters appeared in 1947, used for the first time in Los Angeles for mail delivery. The God's-eye view that the helicopter allowed, hovering with seeming stillness above a famous site, was crucial to the iconizing of the great cities of the world, including of course Hollywood itself.

Do Big Ben and the double-decker bus symbolize London? Does the Eiffel Tower symbolize Paris, the Coliseum Rome, the Empire State Building New York, the Christ of the Andes Rio de

Janeiro? Like the Hollywood sign, they too have become brand names, instantly recognizable signs for the cities that include them, more personal than the glass rectangles of contemporary architecture and the occasional old office building that could be anywhere. Similarly, the destruction of national icons as a motif in apocalyptic films is a shorthand way of indicating the destruction of national values. A pioneer in this method of combining private fears with recognizable public places was Alfred Hitchcock in such films as *Saboteur* (1942, Statue of Liberty) and *North by Northwest* (1959, Mount Rushmore), although none of them were ever destroyed in his films.

Before the re-creation of the sign with sturdier metal letters and more deeply anchored supports, however, others took a hand in making the sign mean something of their own. On January 1, 1976, residents of Hollywood awoke to find the sign now reading "HOLLYWEED." Danny Finegood, a student at California State University at Northridge, had made the transformation as a project in his environmental sculpture class. The assignment was a problem in scale and Finegood created his model, spent about fifty dollars in materials (two pieces of white fabric and two pieces of black to change the "O"s into "E"s), and made the change at night with the help of a few friends. The occasion was the recent passage of a California law decriminalizing the possession of small amounts of marijuana for personal use. Finegood worked his metamorphosis again that Easter, this time by merely blocking out one of the "L"s to create "HOLYWOOD." In later years Finegood often bristled at the charge that what he did was vandalism, or that he was a mere prankster. Like the Pop artists preoccupied by brand names, Finegood considered the sign a piece of sculpture rather than a word, and, by modifying it into another word, he emphasized its plasticity. As Ed Ruscha remarked, "I simply liked the word for its abstract self. . . . I liked that horizontalness."

Later transformations of the sign were less artistically high-minded. The "H" for Hollywood High on a nearby hill that may have helped inspire the original sign acquired a few school-spirit companions in 1978 ("USCWOOD" and "CALTECH"), 1983 ("GO NAVY"), and 1993 ("GO UCLA"). In 1992, despite the installation of a $94,000 closed circuit TV security system, "PEROTWOOD" appeared, in tribute to the third-party presidential candidate, who made a return appearance on the sign in 1996, although the same year the Hollywood Chamber of Commerce vetoed a Disney proposal to repaint the sign with black spots for the remake of *101 Dalmatians*. Finegood himself tried to continue the trend to social relevance with "OLLYWOOD" in the late 1980s, protesting the Iran-Contra testimony of Oliver North, and "OIL WAR" in the early 1990s, against the first Iraq War. Flags have been draped over parts of the sign as well, and people have hung from the letters to publicize causes or just themselves. In late 2001 the homeowners of Hollywoodland had finally had enough. Even with 9/11 in the background, they voted down a proposal to paint the sign red, white, and blue for Veterans Day.

The sign as modified by Danny Finegood for an art project to celebrate the
passing of a marijuana decriminalization law, 1976
(Courtesy of hollywoodpictures.com)

By this time, however, the sign was a permanent fixture in the idea of Hollywood, thanks to the final consolidation of its physical structure in the late 1970s. In 1976 the Hollywood Chamber of Commerce had once again tried to muster enough interest to repair the sign, but by the beginning of 1977, a year after Danny Finegood's "HOLLYWEED" exploit, the money was trickling in and no celebrities had yet offered to participate in a benefit. In January of 1978, frustrated by the lack of activity, two young men, Cory Slater and Stuart Levine, briefly took over the job themselves on a volunteer basis, gathering donations of building material. Congratulated by the Los Angeles Cultural Heritage

Board and saluted by an editorial in the *Los Angeles Herald Examiner* for "a sense of civic spirit we see too little of these days," they insisted that the sign should not be replaced but merely refurbished to its original form.

Later that same year, perhaps shamed by the well-publicized grassroots efforts of Slater and Levine, more prosperous benefactors gave the sign the final shot in the arm that would bring it back to life, albeit in a new form. The most open-handed of these donors were an unlikely group that included no contemporary stars or film studios.[5] First, Hugh Hefner, who had recently relocated the Playboy Mansion from Chicago to Holmby Hills, agreed to host a benefit party at the mansion. But the real kickoff came a month or so later, when Alice Cooper, the heavy-metal musician and goth pioneer (also a recent West Coast transplant), donated $27,777.77 (the Chamber of Commerce benchmark) to reconstruct the final "O" in memory of his friend Groucho Marx, who had died the previous year. Warner Bros. Records then funded the second "O," while Hefner's benefit netted enough (including his own contribution of $30,000) to give him (appropriately) charitable ownership of the "Y," and the singer Andy Williams received the "W." The newspaper publisher Terrence Donnelly signed up for the "H" (for his newspaper the *Hollywood Independent*); Dennis Lidtke, the owner of Gribbit!, a Hollywood graphic design company, took the "D"; and Gene Autry, no longer a singing cowboy star but the owner of the California Angels baseball team as well as station KTLA, opted for the second "L."

Two letters were left begging, and after a time into the breach came an Italian producer named Giovanni Mazza (the first "O") and Les Kelley of Kelley's Blue Book, who had helped fund one of the earlier reconstructions and now received the first "L."

What a disparate collection of rescuers! But perhaps an appropriate one for the checkered history of the Hollywood sign. Spearheaded by Hefner and Cooper, two newcomers to the area with the stardust of old Hollywood still in their eyes, supported by a local newspaper publisher, an automotive pioneer, and the owner of a graphic design company, along with a music publishing company, a former singer turned entrepreneur, and an Italian producer moving to Los Angeles (who seems virtually unknown to the Internet Movie Database). Only Andy Williams stands out as a working performer, singing on the soundtrack of many movies, including, legend has it, dubbing for Lauren Bacall in *To Have and Have Not*. But perhaps that conglomeration of angels is in the nature of Hollywood and the sign as well: outsiders riding to the rescue when the insiders couldn't care less. After all, in the Peg Entwistle story, it took a New Yorker to be the first to see the sign symbolically, and even then it was several decades before others were beginning to catch on.

Whatever the intentions of the sign's new supporters, the money had definitely arrived, and in August 1978 the reconstruction began. City Council members Joel Wachs and Peggy Stevenson, along with Mayor Tom Bradley, smoothed the way for permits, and the Pacific Outdoor Advertising Company, under the supervision of

Hugh Hefner campaigning for the rebuilding of the sign, 1978 (Courtesy of hollywoodpictures.com)

Raiden Peterson, began demolition of the old sign, although the alert visitor can still spot the stumps of its previous incarnation in the shadow of the newer construction. This time, instead of telephone poles for support, it was twenty steel footings, sunk thirteen feet into the slippery soil. Concrete was poured for the foundations, Hughes Helicopter flew in the steel columns, and the letters of corrugated steel with baked white enamel were attached. It cost $250,000, just about the modern equivalent of its original cost, and was finished in less than three months. The configuration of the original sign was followed exactly, including the accurate height of the letters, not the often-claimed fifty, but forty-five feet high. The total weight—foundations, columns, girders, and letters—was 240 tons.

On November 11, 1978, in honor of the seventy-fifth anniversary of Hollywood as a "city of the sixth class," CBS televised a two-hour special, *Hollywood Diamond Jubilee*, to celebrate the sign's completion. Lasers and searchlights illuminated the sign, Raquel Welch and Douglas Fairbanks, Jr., hosted, while Yvonne DeCarlo, accompanied by a thirty-four-piece orchestra, sang Stephen Sondheim's tribute to show business survival, "I'm Still Here," reprising her original part in the 1971 production of *Follies*. The place called Hollywood—the little prohibitionist suburban utopia envisioned by Harvey H. and Daeida Wilcox, H. J. Whitley, Cornelius Cole, Paul de Longpré, and others— had finally merged unquestionably with a temporary advertising sign that had sprung up more than thirty-five years after they came to settle in a bare desert world whose primary landmarks were hills, cactuses, and the occasional dry creek bed. As the first changes of the sign in 1949 were animated by a need to assert Hollywood against its rivals, so the renewal of the late 1970s similarly marks a particular moment in the history of film and Hollywood's self-branding as the "entertainment capital of the world."

With the rebirth of the sign, the decline of Hollywood as an urban area had hardly been entirely stifled. Urban renewal in the form of the Community Redevelopment Authority and federal grants still threatened old landmarks. But a self-consciousness about the Hollywood past had been kindled. Hollywood Heritage, founded in late 1979, took as its first major project an effort to save the Brown Derby restaurant, which had closed and was set to be demolished. A widely publicized campaign stimulated responses from around the country, even though many of the out-of-towners didn't realize that the restaurant with a dome shaped like a hat was on Wilshire Boulevard, while the one most frequented by the stars was a Spanish Mission–style structure on Hollywood Boulevard. In 1980 the hat-shaped Brown Derby was deeded to Hollywood Heritage and the Los Angeles Conservancy, which later arranged for the transportation of its most iconic element to adorn a local mall. At least selectively, old Hollywood was making a feeble comeback, even though by the mid-1980s it was still being referred to as "the film industry's blighted birthplace," and in 1993 Universal City Walk was opened as an antiseptic theme park version of Hollywood Boulevard—a

Four stages of the rebuilding of the sign in 1978
(Courtesy of hollywoodpictures.com)

distant echo of the early journalistic sense that the real center of filmmaking was not in Hollywood but in the San Fernando Valley.[6]

■

Now coming up on the ninetieth birthday of the existence of a sign called Hollywood on Mount Lee, has the re-created sign, itself having passed its thirtieth birthday, finally achieved a kind of permanence? While not as solid as Mount Rushmore or the Grand Canyon, has it finally become stable? I have been tracing the strange ins and outs, ups and downs, of the history of the

Hollywood sign, but perhaps the most crucial thing to be said is that, viewed in the eye of history, the sign is a remarkably durable phantom. Less a word than a metamorphic idea, the sign is cut loose from historical specificity. To say it is "really" an advertising sign is by now meaningless. It cannot be reduced to its origins or even its various resurrections and refurbishings. From Peg Entwistle to Ed Ruscha to Danny Finegood and beyond, the sign has been seen as a symbol, a piece of sculpture, an icon. Towns across the country and around the world announce themselves in the block letters now called the Hollywood Hills font in order to share in its star quality, although the results are usually less celebratory than self-serving announcements of how little they deserve it. But the glamour remains. A friend of mine has told me she saw a replica of the Hollywood sign in Sri Lanka. There's another, it's said, in New Zealand, right near the Sunset Strip Pub, and who knows how many more.

That Los Angeles has been destroyed in films so many times makes practical sense because it's the place where so many films are made. But the cycle of destruction and rebirth also mirrors the phoenix-like history of the Hollywood sign itself. In a sense, the sign had to be remade before it could become iconic, turned from its original purpose into something more general and more abstract. Its impermanence, its rebirths and renovations over time, paradoxically makes it more authentic. As happened to the mythical phoenix itself, destruction and rebirth turns an otherwise ordinary being or object into a concept. Without an understanding of that process, it is hard to explain how a temporary advertising construction of purely local interest became a national and international icon, gathering significance to itself like a snowball rolling downhill, independent of its origins and even its history.

If there had been any actual image there on the hillside, this would not have happened. Being made of only letters allowed the sign to stand outside history, never outdated. Contributing to that sense of eternal if ambiguous meaning is the setting of the sign on a somewhat bleak chunk of hillside, while rising above are the towers, courtesy of Don Lee, of a futuristic communication with the air and the universe. The sign is in a place apart. Just as it has no images that will connect it with a history, its setting is in the timelessness of nature. Its near neighbor, the Hollywood Bowl, was designed as an equally impermanent structure. But the Bowl, unlike the sign, has to be constantly ready for use by musicians and large audiences waiting to hear them, and so now has been reconstructed entirely, adorned with high-definition video screens and the latest in audio technology. The Bowl's changes over the years are thus merely improvements in its function, while the sign, without any immediate or future function, sails grandly in a chariot all its own, still close to nature and the natural (and human) disasters that are also part of the image of Los Angeles.

"Utopia," as coined by Sir Thomas More, can mean either the good place or no place, the best possible place, or a place that does not exist. The Hollywood sign maintains that ambiguity, along with the hazy relation to nature and to culture that exists in both the idea of southern California and the movie business from the start—the desire to build a magic city from raw and seemingly unpromising materials, the ability to see vast potential in a few acres of sagebrush, cactus, and chaparral, like a producer seeing in an otherwise ordinary face the possibility of stardom. The sign functions as a free-floating emblem of that urge and the imagination that underlies it—the mingling of private desire and public space that also characterizes the world of the movies, ostentatiously granting intimacy. Like those first grand mansions with their elaborate gardens that sprang up in early Hollywood, like the Spanish Colonial Revival homes of Hollywoodland that promised an escape from the grimy city, the sign sits in its raw landscape as an intangible promise that Hollywood still has its old meaning, despite all its changes. As Los Angeles develops, and the empty spaces are filled in, it remains an assurance that words and nature, fact and fantasy, are not contrary to each other, but complementary. So many storied places are a letdown when they are finally seen. Hollywood and Vine is just an ordinary street corner. Les Deux Magots, the old existentialist haunt in Paris, is overpriced and the food could be a lot better. Times Square is turning into a bland theme park. Words, images, had infused them with magic. In the flesh they don't quite measure up.

But the Hollywood sign still delivers, perhaps because it can be commandeered by everyone with a camera to mean what they want it to mean. Because it's not a billboard, not flat, its shape is more elusive, with the letters set at odd angles to each other. How you capture it in memory or on film is always a personal choice. For anyone climbing or driving the hills of Hollywood to seek the best road to the sign or the right angle on it, the sign situates you in your own experience. To photograph it or see it enhances your sense of self like seeing a movie star. Unlike fixed icons that may be viewed from different angles but don't really change that much, the sign is a shifting icon whose viewers supply the context, framing themselves and the sign at once.

■

However the Hollywood sign may symbolically stand outside history, it is of course subject to history, whether that means vandals evading the security system to paint on graffiti or developers wanting to steal a little of the magic for their own profit. After the decisive rebuilding of the sign in 1978, something of its aura began to spread to Hollywood itself, no longer the idyllic semi-agricultural community of the Wilcoxes, or even the glittering white way of the 1930s and 1940s, but a place increasingly referred to as "Hollyweird." As one reporter described it in the 1970s, it was a bunch of "active, noisy inner-city streets, littered with the familiar signs of sleaze—pimps, prostitutes, pornography, bars, commercial eyesores, strange people." But with the reconstructed sign as a symbolic magnet, help was on the way. In virtually the same month that the sign was rebuilt, the U.S.

Department of Housing and Urban Development announced a
$90-million-dollar urban-renewal grant, and commercial prop-
erty along Hollywood Boulevard began a slow increase in value
that included the renovation of some of the landmark buildings
of the past, including the El Capitan, Egyptian, Pantages, and
Chinese theaters, as well as the Roosevelt Hotel, which was soon
to sport a swimming pool painted by David Hockney.

More legal stabilization for the Hollywood sign followed its
material reconstruction. In 1988 a young realtor named Chris
Baumgart joined the Hollywood Chamber of Commerce board
of directors and was put in charge of the still somewhat somnolent Hollywood Sign Committee. By 1991 he was head of the
chamber itself, and he spearheaded a long negotiation between
the chamber, the city of Los Angeles, and the state of California
over the ownership of the sign. Much to the city's annoyance, the
negotiations concluded a few years later by assigning all licens-
ing rights to the chamber, with the city owning the land and the
physical sign, and a newly formed nine-member Hollywood Sign
Trust, of which Baumgart was the first and still only chairman, in
charge of repair, capital improvement, and managing the royal-
ties from all of the sign's media appearances. What is specifically
copyrighted about the sign is not the word "Hollywood" or even
the shape of the letters, but their staggered arrangement, their
pitch and toss as they march across the front of Mount Lee. Even
so, there is a distinction, argued legally in each case, whether the
sign is being used as a trademark, in which case a fee has to be

paid, or as a geographic marker to designate a particular part of Los Angeles, which can't be copyrighted. Thus, the glimpse of the sign in the Twentieth Century–Fox logo, added in 1994, gets by without paying any toll to the Chamber of Commerce, whereas the Hollywood Video film rental chain, after a long battle, shelled out its proper assessment.

After the reconstruction and the legal settlement, grand plans to reilluminate the sign, for which donations were already lined up, were thwarted by the real danger of fire, the difficulty of getting fire engines up the winding streets, and the general hostility of the property owners of Hollywoodland. Still, security cameras were installed, insurance against earthquakes and natural disasters was paid for, and in 1995 there was a full-scale repainting of the sign courtesy of the Dutch Boy company, with a celebratory gala hosted by Phyllis Diller, whose face had also been famously refurbished a few times.

The natural setting of the sign also insured that there would be occasional trouble, and not just from interlopers trying to induce the sign to support their own causes. In 1999 lightning destroyed the old security system not long before the sign was to make its appearance as the West Coast icon emblem of the Y2K celebration on December 31, and in 2007 the Griffith Park fire came dangerously close. It is now illegal to hike next to the sign. A razor-wire-topped cyclone fence surrounds the site, and the security system was upgraded in 2005 to include microphones, infrared video cameras, and motion sensors twenty-four hours a day, monitored by the city of Los Angeles from an underground surveillance center. Another repainting, this time funded by Red Diamond, occurred in 2006, and Baumgart estimates this will happen about every ten years, the only seriously needed renovation, in addition to any new security upgrades. Now as well there are two webcams that feed images of the sign to its website, microphones to overhear interlopers, as well as a spy view from outer space, courtesy of NASA's Landsat satellite.

A new crisis, or an opportunity, for the sign—as well as a test for American iconography in general—came in 1997 when President Clinton signed the bill authorizing the minting of commemorative quarters celebrating the fifty states. In 1999 the first, Delaware, appeared, and by summer of 2001 Governor Gray Davis of California appointed a committee to come up with designs for California's contribution. In the usual federal situation different states had different ways of going about the process: in some the governor decided on his or her own; in others there was general consultation. California decided that it would fall to the governor to make a final recommendation, which the U.S. Mint could then modify in accordance with its own needs. But before then anyone in the state could submit designs and recommendations. A committee of experts—scholars, numismatists, artists—headed by California historian and state librarian Kevin Starr would then cut the entries to a hundred, vote and rank the top twenty, and send them to the governor for the final choice.

The sign as the symbol of Hollywood is clear enough, but

what signifies California? Queen Califia, the legendary Amazon ruler of the fictional California, appeared on many designs, as did miners, the Golden Gate bridge, the Del Coronado Hotel, Coit Tower, the condor, palm trees, surfers, Old Faithful, film cans, a cameraman, sunglasses, bears, redwoods, and, of course, the Hollywood sign. Governor Davis chose five to send on to the Mint, including one that featured the Golden Gate Bridge, flanked by palm trees and evergreens, with the Hollywood sign in the background—an admirable effort to pay homage to both northern and southern California. But then something unexpected happened: Gray Davis was recalled in a special election. The new governor was Arnold Schwarzenegger, who quickly pulled back Davis's suggestions from the Mint in order to decide on his own what best symbolized California. In the subsequent discussions, fueled by Schwarzenegger's effort to burnish his environmentalist credentials, Yosemite Valley emerged as the compromise candidate. Advocates argued that it was appropriately in the center of the state (although most would associate it with northern California), and in the quarter issued in 2005 it appears in its most emblematic guise, the Half Dome made famous by Ansel Adams's photographs, accompanied by the figure of John Muir, the early naturalist (another northern California icon), and a California condor, recently returned from near extinction, another "comeback kid." The Hollywood sign, along with all the other persons, places, and things associated with California, would just have to look elsewhere to be symbolically justified.

While all these wranglings over California imagery were going on, another phase in the up-and-down relation between Hollywood and Los Angeles was also in motion. In early 2000, three secessionist movements arose—all in areas annexed or consolidated with Los Angeles by 1915: San Pedro, the San Fernando Valley, and Hollywood. Inside the boundaries of this new Hollywood, according to the proposal, would be the Hollywood Hills and the Hollywood sign. Common to all three secession movements was the perennial feeling, going back to the early years of consolidation, of being shortchanged by Los Angeles in city services, especially, as it seemed from some of the campaign literature, the lax collection of abandoned sofas. Spearheading the Hollywood secession movement was Gene LaPietra, the owner of two nightclubs, and in the eye of history a paradoxical successor to those early Hollywood citizens so intent on keeping noisy industry and movie high jinks away from their palatial homes and quiet streets.

Controversy was immediate, and City Council members in the area, especially Tom LaBonge, focused their outrage on the effort to take control of the Hollywood sign. But the measure qualified for the 2002 ballot, which set off even more back-and-forth accusations, as well as generating an anti-secession movement headed by City Council members LaBonge, Eric Garcetti, and Alex Padilla. Meanwhile, candidates for membership on the prospective Hollywood City Council rushed to file their papers, including Angelyne, a woman whose often scantily clad, pouting, busty image had frequently appeared on Hollywood billboards since the 1980s (paid for by "investors"), and who was once quoted as saying that her fame was pure because she didn't do anything to deserve it except be herself.

But the secession movement was already doomed. The Hollywood Chamber of Commerce, fearful of fiscal uncertainty and undermining current development projects, came out against secession. Practical matters played a role as well, including the difficulty of having a local fire department independent of the city's—an issue that went back to the original decision to consolidate with Los Angeles in 1910. Finally in November 2002, after LaPietra had spent $2.5 million of his own money, all three secessionist movements failed, with Hollywood's losing by more than two to one in the city of Los Angeles, and by only a little less in Hollywood itself.

The campaign for secession may have failed, but the imaginative status of Hollywood as a separate place remained, confirmed legally as a kind of consolation prize in 2006 by the California Assembly, which mandated that Hollywood's official records be kept separate as if it were an independent city. On Hollywood Boulevard as well, even during the secession movement, movie symbolism was still flourishing. In November 2001 the Hollywood and Highland mall, which included a new theater to house the Academy Awards, opened on the former site of the Hollywood Hotel, built just over a hundred years earlier as a resting place for real estate investors and later home sweet home for the occasional film company on location. Intended to be the western anchor of Hollywood renewal, Hollywood and Highland wraps around Mann's (formerly Grauman's) Chinese Theatre. It sits across Hollywood Boulevard from Disney's El Capitan Theater, which had been refurbished earlier, and its main axis is not rectilinear with the intersection but cants northeast—toward the Hollywood sign. Playing on the affinity with the site of the filming of D. W. Griffith's *Intolerance* (in fact some three miles away), the complex features a backdrop of gigantic Assyrian gates with bas-reliefs of winged emperors, and a set of enormous elephants rearing on their hind legs. Thanks to the earmarking of 1 percent for art in new construction, it also includes a witty pathway designed by the artist Erika Rothenberg, titled "The Road to Hollywood: How Some of Us Got Here." As Rothenberg has said, "The problem with public art is that many proposals and finished projects aren't very connected to the site. They're just dropped in. But there's so much history here that the connections are inescapable. The site comes with its own narrative." To enhance that story, she delved into memoirs, oral histories, books, and magazines to come up with a wealth of stories, parts of which are now engraved in thirty-nine panels that make up the path and ten more on other levels of the complex.

But, as so often in Hollywood, nothing happens in a straight line. The path winds around the central plaza, sometimes crossing over itself until it finally comes to rest at the back, where an enormous casting couch sits in an archway that frames the distant Hollywood sign, enhanced by several nearby palm trees. It's the perfect site for a photo op, and the whole project, including the red concrete center of the stairway that rises to the plaza from Hollywood Boulevard, ironically reflects the old myth that anyone can be a star. Once, a growing and optimistic Hollywood had generated a sign that tried, however cautiously, to trade on its glamour. But now the sign, grown old and established, has in its turn become the presiding genius of a renovated Hollywood, intent on recapturing the lure of its own myths. Outside Hollywood and Highland, people dressed as film characters spring up from the street like strange flowers, while Madame Tussaud's next door supplies sidewalk effigies of Marilyn Monroe and Samuel L. Jackson to be posed with as new friends. Even given the daily chaos of the street, one might imagine C. E. Toberman, Sid Grauman, and other early entrepreneurs of the image of Hollywood Boulevard smiling down benevolently.

Still, in the second decade of the twenty-first century, even in 2010, the year that marks the hundredth anniversary of the consolidation of Hollywood and Los Angeles, the permanent place of the sign as unimpeachable icon was not entirely secure. Its stability and celebrity were certainly quite a contrast with the sign's tattered history. The agreement in the early 1990s that gave the Hollywood Chamber of Commerce the rights to the trademark arrangement of the letters, the city of Los Angeles the ownership of the sign and the land it sits on, and the Hollywood Sign Trust the chores of maintenance and security, seemed to be the final word in ensuring the sign's future. But there turned out to be other kinds of threats that security fences can't really prevent, even beyond lightning, wildfires, floods, mudslides, and earthquakes. Oddly, the most recent menace originated in Chicago, where so many of the early film pioneers started before they moved to Los Angeles. This latest looming peril to the sign dated back to 1940, when Howard Hughes bought 138 acres of land to the west of the sign, including Cahuenga Peak, with the intention of building a citadel that, like Mack Sennett's abortive plan of the 1920s, would have panoramic views of both Los Angeles and the San Fernando Valley. The imposing home would be designed for himself and Ginger Rogers, whom he had been dating for a few years. But Rogers, fearful of being locked away "in a hilltop home" and upset at Hughes's flagrant tomcatting, broke up the relationship and made her new home an Oregon dairy farm, leaving Hughes's grand plans as unrealized as Sennett's. Over the years, easements had been granted to the Department of Water and Power to cross the land, and Hughes even won a battle with the city to build an access road, but nothing further was done with the land. Fast forward to 2002, when in a grim forerunner of the 2007 acquisition of the *Los Angeles Times* by the Chicago Tribune Company, the Howard Hughes Trust quietly sold the land to Fox River Financial Resources, a Chicago-area investment firm, for $1,675,000. In 2006, after the land had been divided into four plots destined for luxury estates, having proven that it had legal access to the land, Fox River put the entire parcel on the market for $22 million.

Anger in Los Angeles political quarters was immediate, although with all the subsequent gnashing of teeth no one could be clearly blamed for the city's oversight in not buying the land itself, when it stood fallow all those years. Council member La-Bonge helped bring in the nonprofit Trust for Public Land to assist in appraising the real value of the site. Part of the paradox of the situation was that whatever development went forward would need city permits for utilities, and trucks with construction materials would have to climb steep mountain roads to get to the site, arousing incessant protests from inconvenienced neighbors. Perhaps even more upsetting to prospective wealthy buyers might be that the sign had been viewed as a "soft" terrorist target by Homeland Security. No lives would be lost in the event of an attack there, but any destruction would be a deep cultural shock. Those apocalyptic disaster movies had come home to roost, and it was even said that the Madrid commuter train bombers had images of the sign, along with Disneyland, on their laptops.

With the aid of the Trust for Public Land's negotiations, the price for the property came down to $12.5 million, and a campaign was launched, more widespread than the one that gathered to reconstruct the sign in 1978. For a time the sign itself was draped to say "Save the Peak." It was an interesting publicity move because it made the sign once again unfamiliar to both residents and tourists alike, invoking by its strangeness the specter of what the area would look like with a hodge-podge of luxury housing overshadowing the sign's splendid isolation. During the five days "Save the Peak" was up, a million dollars was raised. This time as well, the studios and the Hollywood powers that be were not so backward in contributing. By early March almost $9.5 million had been raised, from the Motion Picture Academy, CBS, NBC, Sony, Warner Bros., and Time Warner, as well as such individuals as George Lucas, Steven Spielberg, Tom Hanks, and Norman Lear, along with such non-film-related organizations as the Tiffany Company Foundation and the Santa Monica Mountains Conservancy. With $3 million to go, escrow was due to close on April 14, 2010. Then a last-minute reprieve extended the do-or-die date to April 30. The Tiffany Company Foundation and Aileen Getty promised matching grants, and at almost the last minute Hugh Hefner, who with Alice Cooper had helped lead the 1978 reconstruction of the sign, came through with $900,000 more to close the deal. In good silent movie fashion, and almost literally, considering the sign's precarious perch, it was a cliffhanger. Until the next episode at least, "HOLLYWOOD" was saved.

■

Despite all the ongoing real and imaginary threats, from developers, from tourists intent on making their way, from terrorists addicted to symbolic gestures, the Hollywood sign, as yet, sur-vives, now much less susceptible to wind and weather than its original version, bearing the name of the previously dusty suburb that lies below it, now the common term for a whole world of imagination and desire. How appropriate is it as well that this sign that symbolizes Los Angeles, or at least its most famous part, rests near a distinctive summit in the only city in the United States divided by a mountain range.

As local history shows, there has always been a tension be-tween Los Angeles and Hollywood, an embrace of the publicity Hollywood brings and a wariness that this large and complex city will be reduced by being defined by it. Perched high on Mount Lee, the sign emphasizes Hollywood as a place of play, a world in between the real and the fictional, the plain, natural setting, and the glitz it represents. Like Hollywood itself, it's difficult to get to the sign, and the closer you are, the less you can see it whole. The availability of the sign, the pretense of easy access, resem-bles the facade of democratic access to the movies, the incessant media focus that creates what Richard Schickel has called inti-mate strangers, who are in fact, like the sign, themselves almost entirely separate from those who view them. Better to look at the sign from a distance, perhaps from the Griffith Observatory, near the bust of James Dean, with its intriguing inscription in-forming us that Dean was not a rebel but an actor who played one. Such a message tries fruitlessly to resolve the eternal cine-matic confusion between what is real and what is artificial, the useless but compulsory distinction between film and reality. Still the pilgrims come, like those in China who climb the sacred mountains to bask in the aura of the Buddhist and Taoist "immortals," who live for hundreds of years in their lofty, almost inaccessible paradise. Nothing like this was certainly in Harry Chandler's mind when the original sign was built; it was meant to draw paying customers. But still, as in old Hollywood itself, the lure had a touch of paradise about it nevertheless. And as the years went on, it too could become part of the sign's mystique.

What symbolizes a city, where does its essence lie? Newspapers used to be identified with cities, but in the world of the Internet that symbiosis has dissolved. And what of buildings? Urban renewal in Hollywood and downtown Los Angeles, which has had several false starts over the years, now seems finally to have taken hold, with developers and preservationists alike congratulating themselves over the failures of the 1960s and 1970s, because so much of the old stock that gave those areas their flavor wasn't torn down and now could be rehabilitated. In this revitalization, downtown Los Angeles seems quietly bent on a friendly competition with its more famous and internationally recognized suburb, to create its own brand, the un-Hollywood. Frank Gehry's Disney Concert Hall furnished another iconic building, followed by Rafael Moneo's Cathedral of Our Lady of the Angels up the street. At the end of the first decade of the twenty-first century, many movies and television shows seem to have heard the message. Although films such as *Heat, Collateral,*

The Hollywood sign seen from the Griffith Observatory with bust of James Dean

The Soloist, and *(500) Days of Summer*, along with television shows such as *Top Chef Masters* and *Project Runway* in the Los Angeles–based seasons, are set in a recognizable Los Angeles, it is one without the Hollywood sign, the Hollywood Bowl, or the Chinese Theatre. Instead they feature the neo-Chicago look of the new downtown, interspersed with shots of swirling freeways. Even an explicitly set show like *NCIS: Los Angeles* uses the sign, if at all, very sparingly, more interested in finding less familiar locations all around the city.

Perhaps then it is better for this city of multiple cultures to have multiple icons, to be polyiconic or, to use Edmund Wilson's term, "mixturesque." "Hollywood" has always embodied a myth of centralization and coherence tenuously related to the real physical place, an ill-defined but tenacious idea like the promise of movies themselves. Icons like the Hollywood sign can pull together contradictions. In a world now drowning in a sea of billboards and brands, the Hollywood sign remains the prime visual center for a famously amorphous city and industry. The viewer doesn't pass through such icons to another, more spiritual meaning, but stays on their surface, content with the way they gesture at that deeper reality without being too specific about it. Hollywood the industry is now only the third largest producer of feature films in the world, lagging behind both Bollywood (India) and Nollywood (Nigeria). And the number of films actually made in the physical Hollywood continues to drop. In 2008 the state of California produced 31 percent of the feature films made in the United States, a 66 percent drop from 2003. In 2009 there was the steepest year-to-year decline ever, with almost every state in the union offering incentives and tax rebates to lure production. To boost waning local pride and to put pressure on production companies, the *Los Angeles Times* printed a weekly map of area location shooting on its business pages.

Before the Gold Rush, before Hollywood, before the Hollywood sign, Ralph Waldo Emerson, sitting in Concord, wrote of "this new yet unapproachable America I found in the West." It was a metaphor that animated much of the nineteenth-century United States, the push toward the frontier, to the limits, the end of things. Materially the frontier was reached and at least geographically the country settled down. But the urge remained. So too the Hollywood sign, and all it signifies, remains approachable but almost impossible to attain. Despite all the times it has been patched and rebuilt, its physical presence continues to be an imperfect version of its larger meaning, always aspiring, never quite there.

Nevertheless, no matter how many "runaway" movie locations there may be—in the rest of the United States, in Canada, in Eastern Europe, around the world—no matter how many other Hollywoods, Bollywoods, and other-woods may spring up, Hollywood, like the sign, remains the endlessly remade original brand. Other local icons may elbow their way into similar significance—the artistic individualism of Watts Towers, the modernist flying saucer of John Lautner's Chemosphere, the swooping curves of Frank Gehry's Disney Hall. But the Hollywood sign, despite or because of its haphazard history, remains the inescapable eye catcher. Los Angeles and Hollywood have had short histories chronologically, although if their brief years of existence were divided into the real and fictional events that happened there, the number of real and fictional figures that walked their streets, the charismatic density might compete with more ancient and long-lived places. Since its birth as a purely functional commercial message, the Hollywood sign has hardily accrued its charisma over almost ninety years, thanks to chance and fate more than premeditation. Instead of heralding one Hollywood, it celebrates them all, and whatever other dreams its viewers might bring to it. Instead of one moment in time, it evokes time in all its layers, binding the future of Hollywood with its past—presiding from its hillside as the genius of the place, anchoring a world of dreams in 240 tons of concrete and steel—and a name.

Notes

ONE

ONE

Hollywood Before "Hollywood"

1. The Motion Pictures Patent Company, founded in 1908, was a capitulation by several major companies to Edison's incessant litigation (and frequent coercion) against any film company that did not use his cameras. Its exclusive contract with Kodak for film lasted until 1911, and its patent protection expired in 1913.

2. The mass was supposedly celebrated on May 3, 1769, a feast day commemorating the discovery of the True Cross by St. Helena, the mother of Constantine the Great. Unfortunately for the story, the Portolá expedition, which Serra accompanied, did not leave San Diego for the north until mid-July.

3. With his eye on larger claims, Cornelius Cole II is more interested in telling us his grandfather's opinion about Roosevelt, Wilson, Coolidge, and World War I than his connection with this still scrubby part of California.

4. All of these architectural terms are vague and overlapping, as befits an era marked by both architectural eclecticism and a desire among rich patrons to link themselves to as many illustrious forebears as possible through the look of their homes.

5. Previously occupied by A&M Records, the Chaplin Studio is now the home of Jim Henson Productions. Atop the gate is a statue of Kermit the Frog dressed as Chaplin's Tramp.

TWO
Hollywood Becomes "Hollywood"

1. Harold Lloyd's *Movie Crazy* (1932) takes off from the basic plot of *The Extra Girl*: the urge to Hollywood of a Midwesterner, the wrong photo put in an envelope, the letter summoning for a screen test, the misunderstanding, and the mistaken belief he's a dramatic actor when actually he's a natural comedian. Unlike Normand, Lloyd does, however, get a contract as a comedian and doesn't retreat to his small-town home.

2. Another prestigious area in the same vicinity was Fremont Place, in front of one of whose homes the unwed mother played by Edna Purviance leaves the baby destined to become The Kid. The mansion was much later owned by Muhammad Ali.

3. In 1919 McAdoo became the general counsel for the new United Artists combine of Fairbanks, Chaplin, Pickford, and Griffith. He had previously turned down the presidency of the company.

4. My mother-in-law, born in Los Angeles in 1907, recalled Wilshire as a dirt road through the oil fields, but there were also farms as well, as can be seen in the Sennett/Mabel Normand short *The Gusher* (1913).

5. "Slumberland" and "Babyland" had already been used in Forest Lawn Cemetery for the areas of children's graves.

6. The font used resembles one called "Machine," still in use, which according to one typography website was favored in the Midwest in the mid-nineteenth century.

7. Sennett, *King of Comedy*, 262–63.

THREE
Hooray for Hollywood

1. A few years later a story ascribes her suicide to having acted in the "morbid" Myrna Loy film.

2. *Forty-second Street* is set in the New York theater, but its story of the kid from the chorus who becomes an overnight star is pure Hollywood fantasy.

3. McWilliams, *Southern California Country*, 359–60. Neutra quotation from "Homes and Housing," in *Los Angeles: Preface to a Master Plan*, ed. George W. Robbins and Deming L. Tilton (Los Angeles: Pacific Southwest Academy, 1941), 196.
4. Williams, *The Story of Hollywood*, 226.

FOUR
Shadows on the Sign

1. From 1949 to 1952, twenty-five of the top fifty grossing films were westerns, as were a majority of the top prime-time television shows in the decade.

FIVE
From Eyesore to Icon

1. According to one article, Swanson wore the dress from the last scene of *Sunset Boulevard;* another said it was designed for the occasion.
2. Diebenkorn and Hockney had both recently moved to Los Angeles.
3. *The Day of the Locust* film includes a scene of a tour of the sign and a fictional version of the Peg Entwistle story.
4. *Logorama*, which won the Academy Award for Best Animated Short in 2010, continues the apocalyptic use of the sign.
5. A few studios donated services to produce promotional shorts.
6. The 1994 Northridge earthquake irreparably damaged both the original Brown Derby cupola and the Hollywood Boulevard branch.

Bibliography

There are many, many books, both serious and more light-hearted, about Los Angeles and Hollywood. Before listing some that were helpful to me in delving into the history of Hollywood and the sign, I wanted to mention some especially invaluable resources. Kevin Starr's majestic multivolume history of California provides a deep understanding of the state and its different localities and cultures, north and south. Gregory Paul Williams's *The Story of Hollywood: An Illustrated History* (Los Angeles: BL Press, 2005) and his earlier study *The Story of Hollywoodland* (Los Angeles: Papavasilopoulos Press, 1992) are replete with great photographs and insightful comments. The many richly detailed volumes of the History of American Cinema series (Berkeley: University of California Press, 1990–) are a necessary starting place for any investigation of the intricate story of the movies. And last but hardly least, my work on this book was helped immeasurably by the resources available online through ProQuest and its archives of historical American newspapers.

Banham, Reyner. *Los Angeles: The Architecture of Four Ecologies*. Harmondsworth: Penguin, 1971.

Beardsley, Charles. *Hollywood's Master Showman: The Legendary Sid Grauman.* New York: Cornwall, 1983.

Beauchamp, Cari. *Without Lying Down: Frances Marion and the Powerful Women of Early Hollywood.* Berkeley: University of California Press, 1997.

Bengston, John. *Silent Traces: Discovering Early Hollywood Through the Films of Charlie Chaplin.* Santa Monica: Santa Monica Press, 2006.

Blumenthal, John. *Hollywood High: The History of America's Most Famous Public School.* New York: Ballantine, 1988.

Brownlow, Kevin. *The Parade's Gone By . . .* New York: Knopf, 1968.

Buntin, John. *L.A. Noir.* New York: Harmony, 2009.

Chaplin, Charles. *My Autobiography.* New York: Simon & Schuster, 1964.

Clarke, Charles G., A.S.C. *Early Film Making in Los Angeles.* Los Angeles: Dawson's Book Shop, 1976.

Cole II, Cornelius. *Senator Cornelius Cole and the Beginnings of Hollywood.* Los Angeles: Crescent, 1980.

Corning, Evelyn. *Hillside Letters A to Z: A Guide to Hometown Landmarks.* Missoula, Mont.: Mountain Press Publishing, 2007.

Dash, Norman. *Yesterday's Los Angeles.* Miami: E. A. Seamann, 1976.

DeMille, Cecil B. *Autobiography,* ed. Donald Hayne. Englewood Cliffs, N.J.: Prentice-Hall, 1959.

Eberts, Mike. *Griffith Park: A Centennial History.* Los Angeles: Historical Society of Southern California, 1996.

Fogelson, Robert. *The Fragmented Metropolis: Los Angeles, 1850–1930.* Berkeley: University of California Press, 1993.

Grenier, Judson, et al. *Guide to Historic Places in L.A. City.* Historical Society of Southern California, 1978.

Halberstam, David. *The Powers That Be.* New York: Knopf, 1979.

Henstell, Bruce. *Los Angeles: An Illustrated History.* New York: Knopf, 1980.

Isenberg, Barbara. *State of the Arts: California Artists Talk About Their Work.* New York: William Morrow, 2000.

Bibliography

Keyes, Margaret. *Nineteenth-Century Home Architecture of Iowa City* [1948]. Iowa City: University of Iowa Press, 1993.

Koopal, Grace G. *Free Enterprise, Foundation of American Greatness: A Biography of Charles E. Toberman.* 1970 [no publisher or city listed].

Loos, Anita. *A Girl Like I.* New York: Viking, 1966.

Louvish, Simon. *Keystone: The Life and Clowns of Mack Sennett.* New York: Faber, 2003.

McWilliams, Carey. *Southern California Country: An Island on the Land.* New York: Duell, Sloan & Pearce, 1946.

Marion, Frances. *Off with Their Heads: A Serio-Comic Tale of Hollywood.* New York: Macmillan, 1972.

Mathison, Richard R. *Three Cars in Every Garage: A Motorist's History of the Automobile and the Automobile Club in Southern California.* Garden City: Doubleday, 1968.

Morey, Anne. *Hollywood Outsiders: The Adaptation of the Film Industry, 1913–1934.* Minneapolis: University of Minnesota Press, 2003.

Nunis, Doyce B., Jr., ed. *A Southern California Historical Anthology.* Los Angeles: Historical Society of Southern California, 1984.

Olsson, Jan. *Los Angeles Before Hollywood: Journalism and American Film Culture, 1905–1915.* Stockholm: National Library of Sweden, 2009.

Ovnick, Merry. *Los Angeles: The End of the Rainbow.* Los Angeles: Balcony Press, 1994.

Polyzoides, Stefanos, Roger Sherwood, and James Tice. *Courtyard Housing in Los Angeles: A Typological Analysis.* Berkeley: University of California Press, 1982.

Regan, Michael. *Mansions of Los Angeles.* Los Angeles: Regan, 1965.

Robinson, David. *Chaplin, His Life and Art.* New York: McGraw-Hill, 1985.

Robinson, W. W. *Maps of Los Angeles: From Ord's Survey of 1849 to the End of the Boom of the Eighties.* Los Angeles: Dawson's Bookshop, 1966.

Rochlin, Michael Jacob. *Ancient Los Angeles and Other Essays.* Los Angeles: Unreinforced Masonry Studios, 1999.

Ross, Joseph E. *Krotona of Old Hollywood*, vol. 1. Montecito, Calif.: El Montecito Oaks Press, 1989.

Rudd, Hynda L., et al., eds. *The Development of Los Angeles City Government: An Institutional History, 1850–2000*, 2 vols. Los Angeles: Los Angeles City Historical Society, 2007.

Seligman, Donald. *Los Feliz: An Illustrated Early History*. Los Angeles: Los Feliz Improvement Association, 2009.

Sennett, Mack. *King of Comedy*. New York: Doubleday, 1954.

Symons, Allene Kaye. *Boosting the Boom, Taming the Backlash: How the Los Angeles Times Influenced Westward Migration in the 1920s*. Los Angeles, 2002.

Torrence, Bruce T. *Hollywood: The First Hundred Years*. New York: New York Zoetrope, 1982.

Utter, James W. "Territorial Expansion of Los Angeles." Master's thesis, University of Southern California, 1946.

Wanamaker, Marc. *Early Hollywood*. Los Angeles: Arcadia, 2007.

Williams, Gregory Paul. *The Story of Hollywood: An Illustrated History*. Los Angeles, BL Press, 2005.

Wilson, Edmund. *The Twenties*, ed. Leon Edel. New York: Farrar, Straus and Giroux, 1975.

Acknowledgments

With a project like this, that seeks to excavate a history often overlaid with anecdotes and myths, casual comments lead sometimes to blind alleys and sometimes to treasures. Special thanks in that quest go to Amaranth Borsuk, whose researches always turned up more fruitful material than I thought possible.

Chris Baumgart, chair of the Hollywood Sign Trust, along with Betsy Isroelit and Diana Wright, deserve deep appreciation for all their help, as does Leron Gubler, executive director of the Hollywood Chamber of Commerce. In getting the final details of the impending crisis over the Hughes land behind the sign, Council member Tom LaBonge and his communications director Carolyn Ramsay gave freely of their time, as did Paige Rausser of the Trust for Public Land. Thanks too to the open-handed help of Jay Jones and Mike Holland at the Los Angeles and Hollywood archives and to Barbara Hall at the Margaret Herrick Library of the Academy of Motion Picture Arts and Sciences. Thanks as well to Jon Boorstin, Fred Croton, Rick Jewell, Albert Litewka, Raiden V. Peterson, Erika Rothenberg, Corey Slater, Mattie Taormina, Dace Taub, and Steve White.

Index

Index

De Longpre Avenue, 24, 40
Del Rio, Dolores, 89
DeMille, Cecil B., 12, 27, 52, 141
Desert Song, The, 128
De Sica, Vittoria, 130
Diebenkorn, Richard, 157
Diller, Phyllis, 177
Dine, Jim, 156
Disney Concert Hall, 188, 191
Disneyland, 185
Dixon, Thomas, 57
Djakarta Indonesia News, 149
Dr. No, 162
Dodger Stadium, 137
Doheny, Edward L., 55, 64
Donnelly, Terrence, 166
Double Indemnity, 140
Douglas, Kirk, 139
Down Three Dark Streets, 133–34
Dracula, 98
Dragnet, 135
Dressler, Marie, 35–36, 46, 58
Duchamp, Marcel, 9
Dutch Boy company, 177

Earthquake, 161
Easter Parade, 128
Easter Sunrise services, Hollywood Bowl, 6, 65
Echo Park Civic Association, 71
Edendale, Calif., 27–28, 31, 33
Edison, Thomas A., 44, 53, 193n1
Edison Trust, 12, 27, 56, 57
Egyptian Theatre, 60, 89, 176
Eiffel Tower, 8–9

El Capitan Theatre, 176, 182
electric lighting, 77–79, 89
Emerson, Ralph Waldo, 190
Entwistle, Lillian Millicent "Peg," 6, 91–96, 99–100, 109, 161, 167, 172, 195n3
Essanay studio, 33, 34, 40
eugenics, 19–20
Eugenics in New Germany, 20
Evans, Walker, 156
Every Building on the Sunset Strip (Ruscha), 157
Extra Girl, The, 48, 194n1

Fairbanks, Douglas, 50, 54, 58, 60, 78, 105, 194n3
Fairbanks, Douglas, Jr., 169
Famous Players–Lasky, 27, 33, 80
Fante, John, 119, 129–30
Farewell My Lovely (Chandler), 132
Farnum, William, 68
Farrow, Mia, 161
Father Gets into the Movies, 48
Fellini, Federico, 131
"Film Flams," 34, 59
film industry: early reputation of, 12; geography of, 12, 27, 29, 31–33, 39–40, 43–44; in Germany, 44, 56–57; in Japan, 130; legitimization of, 53, 56, 59, 64; technological innovation, 126; wartime effects, 57–58
Film Johnnie, A, 48
film noir, 131–35, 139

206